A Shoddy Detective and the Art of Deception

Mitch Donaldson and Becky Bartram

CW01497131

methuen | drama

LONDON • NEW YORK • OXFORD • NEW DELHI • SYDNEY

METHUEN DRAMA

Bloomsbury Publishing Plc, 50 Bedford Square, London, WC1B 3DP, UK
Bloomsbury Publishing Inc, 1359 Broadway, New York, NY 10018, USA
Bloomsbury Publishing Ireland, 29 Earlsfort Terrace, Dublin 2,
D02 AY28, Ireland

BLOOMSBURY, METHUEN DRAMA and the Methuen
Drama logo are trademarks of Bloomsbury Publishing Plc.

First published in Great Britain 2025

Cover artwork by Rebecca Pitt

A catalogue record for this book is available from the British Library.

Library of Congress Control Number: 2025938731

ISBN: PB: 978-1-3505-8716-8
ePDF: 978-1-3505-8715-1
eBook: 978-1-3505-8717-5

Series: Modern Plays

Typeset by Mark Heslington Ltd, Scarborough, North Yorkshire
Printed and bound in Great Britain

For product safety related questions contact
productsafety@bloomsbury.com.

To find out more about our authors and books visit
www.bloomsbury.com and sign up for our newsletters.

In loving memory of
Paul Donaldson

This show is dedicated to Paul Donaldson, a great father and a great friend, whose belief in this story and in all of us never wavered. He was a constant source of encouragement, humour and heart. His support during the creation of this show meant the world, and though he's no longer with us, his presence is felt in every step we take and every moment we share.

A Note from the Creator

When I first started developing *A Shoddy Detective*, I wasn't trying to reinvent the comedy wheel or the mystery genre, I was just trying to make people laugh. But as the script grew, and rehearsals began and the chaos started to take shape, I realised the show had become something more. It became about community, about creativity and about how much we need to laugh, especially with the people we care about. There's something special about sitting in an audience and hearing your friend, your parent, your sibling, your partner burst out laughing next to you. That moment of shared joy is what I wanted to recreate with this play.

Bringing this story to life has been a team effort in every sense of the word. Our incredible cast, crew and creative team over the years have poured their energy and creativity into every moment. They've helped shape these characters and this world into something far more hilarious, heartfelt and ridiculous than I could have imagined on my own. It's one thing to imagine a scene in your head at 2 am; it's another to watch a group of brilliant, committed actors bring it to life and make it better.

Live theatre is a special kind of magic. It's about sharing a space with others, letting go for a little while, and laughing together, loudly, often and without apology. That's the feeling I wanted to create with *A Shoddy Detective*: the joy of watching something a little silly, a little chaotic and a whole lot of fun with the people who matter most. None of this would have been possible without the overwhelming support from our families and our friends. Whether it was helping us haul set or props around, listening to us trial some questionable jokes, or just being there when we needed a good rant or a good laugh, the encouragement has meant everything. Thank you for believing in this show and in us.

This show also carries something deeply personal with it. My father, who passed away in July 2024, was one of our biggest supporters. He believed fiercely in the show, in this company and in the joy that laughter can bring to people's lives. His encouragement, humour and heart are woven into every part of this play. This is for him, too.

Thank you.

A huge thank you to Josh, Matthew and Huw, for taking a chance on a relatively unknown company and helping us grow as creatives. Your trust and support have meant the world.

To Holly, Adam and ASH, you've been integral to the heart of Shoddy from the very beginning. Thank you for giving up your time in those early, chaotic stages and for helping shape us into who we are today.

To Becky, thank you for being an absolute rock throughout this process. Your support, humour and 'level-headedness' have made this whole journey not just possible, but genuinely joyful. I'm so glad you're part of it.

And finally, to Mam, Tait, Cole, Granda and of course to all our in-laws, aunties, uncles, cousins and friends, thank you for the love, the encouragement and the unwavering support over the years. We truly wouldn't be where we are without you.

I hope you read with a lighter heart and maybe a sore stomach from laughing.

I wish you all the best for the future and I certainly hope it isn't too Shoddy . . .

Mitch Donaldson

CAST AND CREATIVES

ACTOR | NEIL JENNINGS

Neil is no stranger to this high energy style of comedy, having been part of the Pantaloons Theatre Company for over twelve years. His comedy chops have seen him showing the world his Bottom and his Benedick, as well as Not Doing that Lake Bit as Mr Darcy, and contemplating which utensil hurts more as the Sheriff of Nottingham.

He is also one half of the founders of Mangled Yarn Theatre Company, whose debut show was *Frankenstein the Pantomime,* where Neil played the Dame Mrs F, and most recently a madcap take on *It's a Wonderful Life*, where Neil played George Bailey. Mangled Yarn have been lucky enough to have spent two years taking their shows to Copenhagen and are set to take *A Christmas Carol* there this December.

Neil also regularly plays the Dame in numerous pantomimes across the country, most recently Widow Twanky with Big Little and Nurse Nora in Hyjack's *Sleeping Beauty* at Trinity Theatre, Tunbridge Wells.

TV credits include *EastEnders, Call the Midwife* and the BSL channel's first ever deaf sitcom *Coffee Morning Club*, as Sergeant Simpson.

ACTOR | WESLEY GRIFFITH

Wesley trained at the Guildford School of Acting (2010).

His stage credits include: Romeo in *Romeo and Juliet* (UK tour, Miracle Theatre); Algernon in *The Importance of Being Earnest* (UK tour, Miracle Theatre); Moriarty in *The Death of Sherlock Holmes* (UK tour, Miracle Theatre); Sam in *Cornwall Vs China* (The Vaults/The Old Red Lion, All the Pigs); Mellors in *Not: Lady Chatterley's Lover* (Theatre503/ Edinburgh Fringe/UK tour 2018 and 2021, Happy Idiot); *My Paper Girlfriend* (one person play, Brighton Fringe); Jimmy in *Dinner is Coming* (The Vaults); Colonel Mustard in *Cluedo* (national tour); Chris in *Windfall* (Southwark Playhouse).

Wesley has also appeared in film/commercials such as: Jay in *The Gym* (Kayvan Novak, BBC pilot); Finnair, July (TV/internet); *Kellogg's, Chocoholic* (TV/internet); Ben in *Starbucks Red Cup* (internet); Diageo (internet); Tarzan in *Vicks Lozenges* (Europe); Conran in *Meet the Richardsons* (Dave, UKTV).

WRITER, PRODUCER & ACTOR | MITCH DONALDSON

Mitch Donaldson is an actor and theatre all-rounder from Northumberland, who trained at the National Youth Theatre and East 15 Acting and Stage Combat, where he set up Shoddy Theatre upon graduating.

Mitch produced Shoddy's work which sold out at the Camden Fringe, New Normal Festival, Edinburgh Fringe and the 2023 spring tour. In 2023, he was selected as part of the cohort for Mercury Theatre producers' scheme. As a performer his theatre credits include: *A Shoddy Detective* (Shoddy Theatre); *Blyth Spirit* (Live Theatre, Newcastle); *Romeo and Juliet* (Globe Theatre, Rome); *A Night Before Christmas* (Theatre N16) and *Simon Boccanegra* (Royal Opera House). Mitch also directed and produced the UK tour of *The Olive Boy* which won an Offie in 2025.

WRITER, ACTOR & COMPANY MANAGER | BECKY BARTRAM

Becky is an actor and stunt performer from Yorkshire, and a graduate of the East 15 Acting and Stage Combat course.

She joined Shoddy Theatre in 2020 and is now the company manager. Stage credits include: *A Shoddy Detective* (Shoddy Theatre); *Dragon Slayer* (Knights of Middle England); and *Unacceptable* (Vienna English Theatre).

TV special action credits include: *The Witcher: Blood Origin* (Netflix); *The Witcher* S3 (Netflix); *Sandman* (Netflix); *Gangs of London* (ITV); *Citadel* (Amazon); and *Slow Horses* (Apple TV).

Stage manager credits include: *Dear Santa* (NLP Productions); *Atom & Luna* (Matthew Linley Creative Projects); *As SHE Likes It* (Chloe Wade Productions); and *The Olive Boy* (Mitch Donaldson Creative). Becky is currently training for the British Stunt Register.

UNDERSTUDY | ALEXANDRA RICOU

Alexandra is an actor and writer.

They trained at Mountview and, since 2021, have been a member of the award-winning street theatre company, the Natural Theatre Company.

Theatre credits include: *A Christmas Cracker* (Natural Theatre Company); *Gluck's Flowers* (Theatre West); *I KILLED MY EX* (Dear Dark Productions); and *The Wind in the Willows* (Calf2Cow).

On screen, they recently starred in the award-winning short film, *Queer Enough*, which screened as part of the BAFTA-qualifying Iris Prize.

SET & COSTUME DESIGNER | LOUIE WHITEMORE

Louie is an Olivier-nominated set and costume designer whose work spans theatre, ballet and opera as well as installations and site-specific productions. Originally from the Lake District, she has worked around the country and abroad, with productions in Germany, Italy and Lithuania as well as further afield in America, China, Pakistan and Palestine.

SOUND DESIGN | SAM BAXTER

Sound design includes: *Why I Stuck a Flare Up My A**e For England* (Southwark Playhouse, UK tour, Edinburgh Fringe, Adelaide Fringe); *You Are Going to Die* (Southwark Playhouse); *A Manchester Anthem* (Vaults and Edinburgh Fringe); *Putrid Beauty* (Actors East); *The Cosmonauts Last Message . . .* (Oxford School of Drama).

PRODUCTION MANAGER & LIGHTING DESIGNER | ADAM JEFFERYS

Adam is a lighting designer and production manager from Essex.

He has been a part of Shoddy since their inception in 2018, working with his close friends Becky and Mitch. Alongside this he predominantly works within new writing; recent credits include: *Speed*, *Statues*, *My Father's Fable* and *Elephant* (Bush Theatre); *Animal Farm* (UK tour); *The Bleeding Tree* (Southwark Playhouse); and *After the Act* (New Diorama).

For his work visit his website: www.adamjefferys.com

ASSISTANT SET & COSTUME DESIGNER | JESSICA STANTON

Jessica is a set and costume designer, and an associate designer. This is her second production working for Louie as an associate designer, the first being *Suite in Three Keys* at the Orange Tree Theatre.

HEAD OF MARKETING & ASSOCIATE PRODUCER FOR SHODDY THEATRE | HOLLY SALEWSKI

Holly is a Bristol-based marketing director and promoter, putting bums on seats and helping people create lasting memories since 2019. Previous show marketing includes: *Just My Imagination* (UK tours); *Rat Pack* (UK tours and Adelphi Theatre, West End); *The Wizard of Oz* (KD Productions, UK tour). The 2025 *Shoddy Detective* tour has been a personal and professional highlight, made even better by working with her pals.

For more of Holly's work visit: www.hollysalewski.com

EXECUTIVE PRODUCER | HUW ALLEN

Huw is a theatrical producer who has worked extensively within the theatre, media and entertainment world for over a decade. He is a founding member of the National Theatre's Young Studio and has produced work commercially with some of the world's leading creative visionaries, with names such as Matthew Vaughn, Tom Hooper, Martin Scorsese, Martin Campbell and Tom Ford. Huw is credited with producing some of the most groundbreaking, innovative and commercially successful campaigns for Google, Apple, Samsung and the BBC over the past fifteen years, earning him a D&AD award for creative excellence in 2019.

Huw served as executive producer on *A Shoddy Detective and The Art of Deception* (UK tour); *A Shoddy Christmas Carol* (Lichfield Garrick Theatre); Tony and Olivier award-winning *ART* by Yasmina Reza starring Seann Walsh (UK tour); and co-producer on Sebastian Faulks' *Birdsong* (UK tour and Alexandra Palace); *The Croft* by Ali Miles (UK tour); and *Murder at Midnight* by Torben Betts (UK tour).

PRODUCER | SHODDY THEATRE

Back in 2018, a small group of graduating East 15 Acting School students were partnered together for their final assessment project which was to devise and create a play entirely on their own. Opting for a comedy as a way of enjoying their final few weeks, the group agreed to create a multi-rolling, slapstick piece, inspired by the classics of British and American comedies. Set in a manor home when a priceless painting goes missing, their first performance of *The Art of Deception* was a hit, receiving outstanding feedback and resulting in many of the audiences returning throughout its four-day run.

As a result, the company was awarded the Essex University Graduate Grant to take the show further and become a professional theatre company, which is where Shoddy Theatre was born.

Since being established, Shoddy have sold out their runs at the Camden Fringe, New Normal Festival and a 2023 spring tour. Their first run at the Edinburgh Fringe in August 2022 caused a huge buzz around town and sold out for the majority of its run.

In 2022, Shoddy were also awarded Arts Council funding for their work in bringing theatre to low socio-economic areas in England. This is the one of the many ways Shoddy aim to make theatre accessible to all, regardless of their backgrounds. Due to the success of previous campaigns, Shoddy received further funding in 2023 to produce a UK tour of *A Shoddy Detective* which sold out for the majority of its run, providing the opportunity for Shoddy to cement itself as an emerging theatre company. Shoddy have now created two further productions, *A Shoddy Lamplighter* and *A Shoddy Christmas Carol* . . . coming soon.

Shoddy also produced the Edinburgh Fringe hit show, *The Olive Boy*, directed by Mitch Donaldson, which was nominated for three Offie Awards, and won Best Creation in 2025.

PRODUCER | THE PRODUCTION GARDEN

Producer: Joshua Beaumont
Associate Director & Producer: Matthew Emeny
Production Coordinator: Mirella Lloussi

The Production Garden is an award winning theatre and event production company co-founded by Joshua Beaumont and Matthew Emeny.

TPG productions include: Tony and Olivier Award winning *ART* by Yasmina Reza starring Seann Walsh (UK tour); *Pride and Prejudice* (*Sort Of)* by Isobel McArthur (CAA, Toronto, North American premiere); *Awake My Soul: The Mumford and Sons Story* (UK tour); *Why I Stuck A Flare Up My A**e For England* (2025 Offie Award Winner, Adelaide Fringe Award Winner, Holden Street Theatre Award Winner, Southwark Playhouse, UK tour, Australia); Sebastian Faulks' *Birdsong* (UK tour and Alexandra Palace); *A Shoddy Detective and the Art of Deception* (UK tour); *A Shoddy Christmas Carol* (Lichfield Garrick Theatre); *Jenny Ryan: Out of the Box* (UK tour); co-producer on *The Croft* by Ali Miles (UK tour); and *Murder at Midnight* by Torben Betts (UK tour).

Forthcoming productions include: Ben Weatherill's *Motorhome Marilyn* starring Michelle Collins, premiering at the Edinburgh Fringe Festival 2025; *Parody of the Rings* (Edinburgh 2025); Michael Morpurgo's *Private Peaceful* adapted and directed by Simon Reade (UK tour); James Kettle's *Chaplin*, starring Seann Walsh.

The Production Garden also creates theatrical events including the Garden Theatre Festival – Bath's only outdoor theatre event, presenting a repertory theatre company bringing classic plays to a bespoke 400-seat theatre every summer to the gardens of the Holburne Museum and Father Christmas' Grotto at Milsom Place, Bath.

ASSOCIATE PRODUCER | MERCURY THEATRE

The Mercury is an artistic powerhouse in the East – a vital, vibrant, welcoming centre of culture for the people of Colchester, Essex and beyond.

The theatre takes its name from the Roman messenger god, Mercury.

It was Mercury's task to connect the people with the gods, and so, in keeping with our name, connection is at the heart of everything we do.

www.mercurytheatre.co.uk

A Shoddy Detective and the Art of Deception is developed and adapted by Mitch Donaldson and Becky Bartram from *The Art of Deception* by Mitch Donaldson, Josh Thompson, Zach Devereux, Lucy Wordsworth, Nick Mulvey and Megan Froud.

A Shoddy Detective and
the Art of Deception

Characters

Lord Henry Raeburn
Lady Penelope Raeburn
Detective Stuart Pidcock
Chief Constable Sweetheart
Dusty Wills
Nora (Maid)
Bertha (Cook)
Mick (Gardener)
Roy (Gardener)
Richard Wymore
Mary Wymore
Anastasia Bramavich (Russian Heiress)

Act One

Scene One

The Great Hall of Raeburn Manor, the walls are covered in dark wood panelling, with wall sconces, creating a pleasant yet sophisticated ambience. There are doorways either side of the room. On the walls there are portraits of the Raeburns' relatives, however one of the paintings is missing a plaque. There are different ornaments around the room as well as a wall-mounted sword and shield.

Downstage right: a radio and a lamp are perched on a writing desk. On the wall next to it is a wall-mounted telephone.

Upstage right is a drinks trolley and a standing lamp next to a bay window, with curtains.

Upstage centre is a fireplace with ornaments; above it is a covered picture frame. Next to the fireplace is a fireside set containing a fire poker.

At centre stage is a lounge chair and footstool with a side table.

Upstage left features another large bay window and curtains, with a side table featuring a lamp and another telephone. A chair sits by the side of the table.

Downstage left is a plant pot stand.

Lights dim.

Enter **Lord Henry Raeburn, Lady Penelope Raeburn** *and* **Detective Stuart Pidcock**.

Lord Raeburn, *middle-aged, pretentious and full of himself. He is very polished and suave, and is dressed eloquently in a tweed suit.*

Lady Raeburn, *middle-aged, sophisticated and regal. She is more humble in her upbringing and does not boast about wealth.*

Pidcock *is a bumbling detective, his clothes and hat are smart but worn and ill fitting. He has a positive outlook on life, although he is positive you get the sense that he always seems lost and despite his bumbling nature things conveniently fall into place for him.*

Lord Henry Raeburn, Lady Penelope Raeburn *and* **Detective Pidcock** *are greeting each other in the space, having general small talk as they walk towards the audience.*

Lights up.

Raeburn   Ladies and gentlemen! Hello and welcome to Raeburn Manor, for the Raeburn charitable ball. I am, of course, your host for the evening, Lord Henry Raeburn (*Beat, wait for the audience to react poorly.*) . . . (**Raeburn**'s *disappointed, repeats it again, awaits bigger applause.*) Joining us this evening is my . . . darling wife, Lady Penelope Raeburn.

Penelope   Oh, thank you, thank you, it is such a terrific turn out, I am really quite speechless /

Raeburn   / Well yes, darling, that is probably for the best.

They laugh before intensely staring into each other's faces.

We are also extremely privileged to be joined this evening by the man who famously caught the world renowned thief Dustin Wills. Please welcome, Detective Stuart Pidcock . . .

Pidcock   Thank you, thank you. I wrote a little something down for the occasion, if you don't mind . . .

Raeburn   By all means, Detective.

Lord Raeburn *applauds* **Pidcock** *as he fumbles around in his pockets before pulling out a piece of paper . . .*

Pidcock   'It's an honour to be here this evening.'

Beat. **Pidcock** *puts his note away.*

Raeburn   Yes, the honour's all ours, Detective. Now tell us, what was it like capturing the biggest criminal in the world?

Pidcock It wasn't easy, they are an incredibly conniving crook. I sacrificed a great deal, countless sleepless nights and stake-outs, tracking and surveillance. I put my blood, sweat and tears into capturing them until finally, after years of searching . . . finally . . .

Raeburn You captured them?

Pidcock They turned themselves in.

Raeburn What?

Pidcock But tonight isn't about me, it's about your auction and the priceless painting.

Raeburn Yes, the Detective is correct, as today we will be auctioning off the finest, most exquisite work of art, *El Arte del Engaño.*

Penelope English, darling.

Raeburn *The Art of Deception.* Kindly donated by an incredibly generous and modest gentleman . . . me (*Gestures audience for an applause.*) No, no, no need to thank me, I'm just doing my bit to help the poor and needy in the community, you're welcome. It is lovely to have you all with us and of course so refreshing to welcome back familiar faces, as well, hello madam. It is lovely to welcome you back, and of course with your usual tipple in hand, I see. Well, you know as they say, 'when in Rome' . . . And everywhere else in your case. May I suggest you go easy on the alcohol this evening, we don't want a repeat of last time do we? Just remember that clothing must be worn at all times.

Penelope Now, as well as having some familiar faces, it's lovely to welcome some new faces. Hello madam, may I say you look simply ravishing this evening and sir, you look . . . Yes, well, thank you both for coming.

Raeburn In fact, thank you all for coming, whether it be familiar faces, new faces, whatever kind of face that is and (*Shocked.*) some rather disgraced faces. My goodness, sir, you have a nerve showing your face around here, didn't think I'd notice you but I've read the papers – 'Disgraced Surgeon' caught sleeping with one of your patients, I believe, damn shame . . . as you were one of the best vets in town.

Pidcock *and* **Lady Raeburn** *tut in disgust.*

Raeburn   Anyways, it's time for the moment you have all been waiting for. If you two could kindly do the honours. Ladies and gentlemen, for the first time, before your very eyes, the rare, the exquisite, and some would say priceless painting. Christiano De La Main's masterpiece, *El Arte del Engaño.*

Penelope   English, darling.

Raeburn   *The Art of Deception.*

The painting is revealed but the frame is empty – gasps all round.

I know, it's breathtaking, isn't it, sometimes the simplest of things can make tremendous – AHHH, it's gone! It's gone! . . .

The lights flicker frantically as they all begin to panic.

Pidcock *moves to C/S and begins to look around. A spotlight highlights* **Pidcock***.*

Pidcock   Bloody hell, nobody move! Lock the doors! Close the curtains! No one is allowed leave!

Radio begins to play a collage of news bulletins about the recent theft. They all blame **Pidcock***'s ineptitude.*

Newsreporter One   Aye, when I heard the news I couldn't quite believe it. I was like, howay man, what are you doing like?

Newsreporter Two   He has fumbled another case.

Newsreporter Three   Detective Pidcock is an absolute embarrassment.

Newsreporter Four   Detective Pidcock should be ashamed of himself.

Newsreporter Five   I'm not surprised to hear about that British buffoon.

The radio and lights stop with **Pidcock** *C/S.*

Pidcock   Oh no, not again!

Blackout.

Scene Two

Radio is on, discussing the recent events.

Newsreporter (*on radio*)   Shock in the home counties, the world renowned painting *The Art of Deception* by Christiano De La Main has been stolen. This is in spite of the attendance of Scotland Yard's so-called finest detective, Stuart Pidcock, who was utterly powerless in his attempts. We are joined by our chief reporter and world renowned criminologist, Dr Seymore Stuffnicked. Dr Stuffnicked, can you tell us the current proceedings in Raeburn Manor?

Lights begin to fade up.

As the radio plays **Pidcock** *happens to be doing the exact same movements the radio narrates on.*

Dr Stuffnicked (*on radio*)   Thank you for having me, I can indeed give you the latest updates. No doubt that Detective Pidcock will be pacing around the room as we speak, feeling an overwhelming sense of embarrassment. He will be scratching his head and rubbing his chin in confusion. I won't mention the fiasco with notorious thief, Dusty Wills. He will probably be tempted to pour himself a large drink, but he'll stop, he'll then go to pour and stop again. He will continue to pace around the room, searching for answers and possible clues, maybe behind a curtain perhaps. I don't blame his frustration as he has fumbled yet another case. Bless you. It wouldn't surprise me if he made his way to the radio and turned it / . . . off

Pidcock *turns off the radio and stares at it in confusion. He lets a deep breath out.*

Suddenly the phone rings. **Pidcock** *is shocked, he reluctantly goes over to answer it.*

Pidcock   Hello? . . . Oh, it's only you, Sweetheart. (*Reassuringly.*) Sweetheart, stay calm. Don't worry . . . I know there's a lot of people talking but I have this under control . . . I will probably be staying at work late. I'm at the manor now. (*Alarmed.*) What? You're coming here? Now? Sweetheart, that won't be necessary . . . yes? . . . Yes but I really don't think you need to be here . . . Hello? Hello, Sweetheart? . . . Oh no.

Enter **Chief Constable Sweetheart**, *a large authoritative figure, loud, intimidating and Scottish.*

Pidcock   Sweetheart?!

Sweetheart   That's Chief Constable Sweetheart to you, Pidcock! What in the world are you playing at?

Pidcock   Nothing, sir.

Sweetheart   I thought putting you in charge of guarding a priceless piece of art would be a simple task that not even you could mess up.

Pidcock   It's not that bad, Sweetheart, honest.

Sweetheart   You're an embarrassment, a disgrace. How could you let someone steal something under your very nose.

Sweetheart *takes an ornament off the mantelpiece and examines it before putting it in his pocket.*

It seems like this is out of your control now!

Pidcock   But Sweetheart, I have this all under control.

Radio turns itself on.

Newsreporter (*on radio*)   I think we can all agree that Detective Pidcock does not have this under control.

Pidcock *switches it off, laughing awkwardly.*

Pidcock   Oh, take no notice of that, Sweetheart.

Sweetheart   Clearly I was wrong, now the whole world knows of your mistake.

Pidcock   Please, Sweetheart, I think that's a bit of an exaggeration. The whole world doesn't know about this.

Radio turns itself on.

French Newsreporter (*on radio*)   The foolish Detective Pidcock has, as they say in England 'made another cock up'. Hu Hu Hu Hu.

Pidcock *switches the radio off aggressively.*

Pidcock   Please, Sweetheart, just give me another chance. I swear to you I will find this painting.

Sweetheart   Oh you've got that right, Detective, but I think you're gonna need a partner to help solve the case.

Pidcock   A partner?! Nothing of the sort!

Radio turns itself on.

Newsreporter (*on radio*)   It's quite clear that Detective Pidcock is in need of a partner.

Pidcock *switches the radio off aggressively.*

Pidcock   Don't do this to me, Sweetheart.

Sweetheart   I'm sorry, Pidcock, but you have left me with no choice.

Pidcock   But I don't need a partner!

Pidcock *preempts the radio switching on . . . nothing.*

He turns back to **Sweetheart**.

Radio turns itself on.

Newsreporter (*on radio*)   He does.

Pidcock *thumps the top of the radio.*

Newsreporter (*on radio; beat*)   Ouch.

Sweetheart   You will be assisted by none other than your old nemesis, Dustin Wills.

Enter **Dusty Wills**, *attractive, suave, charming, wearing a hat.*

Pidcock   What?!

Sweetheart   If you're to catch a thief, you must think like one too.

Pidcock   You're releasing a criminal I spent many years trying to put behind bars?

Dusty   But you never caught me, did you, Pidcock?

Pidcock   That's Detective Pidcock to you, Dustin.

Dusty   My friends call me Dusty.

Pidcock   Well then, you won't mind if I call you Dustin.

Dusty   Oh, we're gonna make a great team, don't you think, Detective?

Pidcock   I think a lot of things.

Dusty   First time for everything I suppose, old boy.

Pidcock   But, but, but Sweetheart . . .

Sweetheart   No BUTS! The pair of you will have to get along. Pidcock, if you solve the case you will restore your reputation and be promoted to Detective Chief Inspector Pidcock, now how does that sound?

Pidcock   Detective Chief Inspector Stuart Pidcock, it has always been my dream, sir . . .

Sweetheart   And you, Dusty Wills, well, you will be given shorter sentence.

Dusty   Now hold on a second, old chap, you're going to have to do better than that.

Sweetheart   Oh is that so? (*Aside to* **Pidcock**.) Watch this, Pidock, this is a classic case of negotiating but you must keep your integrity. Right, so what do you propose?

Dusty   How about, *when* I solve the case, I get my freedom.

Sweetheart   I WILL NOT BE BRIBED.

Dusty   I'll also split the reward money.

Sweetheart   You have yourself a deal.

They shake hands.

You see that, Detective, integrity. Do not lose yourself in the midst of all this, you've got to remain true to yourself, do not lose your character (*In an Irish accent.*) because when you lose character it looks very unprofessional to those around you and they begin to question what on earth you're doing. (*Back to Scottish.*) So remember that, Detective, do not lose character. Now, the pair of you, get to work!

Pidcock   But Sweetheart, there must be another way.

Lights fade.

Scene Three

Scene change to Raeburn Manor, afternoon, jaunty music plays as **Penelope** *enters the space. She looks around the room before making her way to the phone and dialling a number.*

Music fades.

Penelope   Hello, hello? Yes, is that you? Hello, darling, don't worry we're all alone now, it's just you and me. I hear you've got something for me. Oh, you naughty devil, stop it, no go on. Nothing can stop us now.

Knock at the door.

Oh bother, just a minute! (*To the phone.*) No, not you, I'm sure you can go longer . . . I hear someone's been a bad boy!

Pidcock *and* **Dusty** *enter, tussling with each other to get through the door first.*

Pidcock   Yes you could say that, someone stole a priceless painting.

Penelope *is startled.*

Penelope   Oh, Detective, I am sorry, I was just on an important phone call, but I will call them back.

Pidcock   Not at all, if it's important then please finish off.

Penelope   What?

Pidcock   Your phone call.

Penelope   Oh, the phone call, no it's not that important really, it's just the local . . . delivery man.

Pidcock   Nonsense, a woman of your status, everything is important, please continue . . .

Penelope (*hesitantly*)   Hello, yes, I'm sure you do . . . well I look forward to receiving your . . . package very soon . . . What? . . . Well you'll just have to wait . . . I don't know . . . have a cold shower. (*Slams phone down.*) Apologies for the lack of hospitality, we're just so short of staff these days.

Pidcock   That's quite alright.

Penelope   Why, just the other day we were forced to sack our kitchen porter.

Pidcock   Sack? My goodness, whatever the devil for?

Penelope   Well, you see, she was constantly riding the dumb waiter . . .

Pidcock   Well at least the dumb waiter still works?

Penelope   No, he was sacked as well . . . And who might this be?

Dusty   I'm Wills . . . Detective Dusty Wills.

He smirks towards **Pidcock**.

Penelope   Wait, you're *the* Dusty Wills? The notorious thief, Dusty Wills? Oh my pleasure, Penelope Raeburn.

Dusty   No, my lady, the pleasure is all mine.

Kisses her hand, she is taken away by it.

Pidcock   Would you be so kind as to inform the lord of the manor of our presence?

Penelope   Yes, he's in his study, I'll send for him. In the meantime, please make yourself comfortable and I'll have Maid Nora bring you some tea.

Dusty   Till we meet again.

Dusty *blows her a kiss, she flutters off stage.*

Beat.

Pidcock   What on earth do you think you're doing? That is the lady of the manor, have some respect.

Dusty   What? A chap can't have a little fun on the job, Detective?

Pidcock   You're not here to have fun, you're here to catch a criminal. Remember, *if* you help us solve the case, you're a free man. But if you don't, then I will pull you off this case and I will enjoy marching you straight back to your cell.

Pidcock *squares up to* **Dusty**.

Dusty   You wouldn't dream of pulling me off this case.

Pidcock   Oh, you really think I won't pull you off?

Nora *enters. The maid of the house. Sweet, kind and withered, her time at Rayburn Manor has taken a toll on her. Loyal, helpful and caring.*

Dusty   I know you won't pull me off.

Pidcock   I've wanted to pull you off since we became partners.

Dusty   Is that so?

Pidcock   In fact, I'll pull you off right now!

Nora *is shocked and uncomfortable.*

Nora   Oh, I am sorry if I am interrupting.

Pidcock   Not at all, you aren't interrupting a thing. I'm Detective Pidcock.

Dusty   And I'm his partner, Detective Wills.

Nora   Oh, your partner, how lovely . . . I'll be honest, we don't see many of your lot around.

Dusty/Pidcock   Oh what, us two? No. It's not like that.

Nora   But don't you worry, your secret is safe with me. Now, can I get either of you a cup of tea?

Pidcock   Don't trouble yourself.

Nora   Don't be silly, it's no trouble at all! Let me see, milk and one sugar.

Dusty   You're all the sweet I need.

Nora (*giggling*)   Oh, Detective Wills. You are a lucky man, Detective.

Nora *exits.*

Pidcock   You just can't help yourself, can you?

You just enjoy your freedom whilst you can. Meanwhile, the real detectives will do the real work.

Dusty   What real work, pray tell?

Pidcock   Like finding out information about this painting!

Dusty   You mean *El Arte del Engaño, The Art of Deception* by Christiano De La Main, his last painting before his death in 1772. A very moving piece . . .

Pidcock (*mocking*)   A very moving piece . . . Would you just stop!

Dusty   Stop what?

Pidcock   Impersonating an officer! Seducing the suspects! Pretending to be interested in art! Now can we get back to work.

Dusty   Detective, old boy, in any great Dusty Wills caper, there is always a level of charm needed in order to gain information. Try being slick, debonair, charming.

Dusty *leans against the wall.*

Pidcock   Don't make me laugh! What makes you so charming?

Dusty   Well, can I be frank with you, Detective?

Pidcock   You can be whoever you want to be but it won't make you anymore charming, Frank.

Dusty   No, that's not what I meant.

Pidcock   And quite frankly, Frank, I can be just as charming and as slick as you.

Pidcock *goes to lean against the door as* **Lord Raeburn** *enters, and falls through it.*

Scene Four

Raeburn   Afternoon gentlemen, apologies for keeping you waiting for so long but this place seems to be getting larger and larger.

Pidcock *stumbles up.*

Pidcock   Yes, that's not a problem, this is an incredibly large home you have here.

Raeburn   Ah yes, yes, she's a beauty. Been in the family for generations. Built by the great Sir Nicholas Hall in 1666, she features seventeen bedrooms, twelve bathrooms, a servants' quarters and a three-storeyed library.

Beat.

Pidcock   Three stories? Hardly many books for a library. But anyway, this is Dustin /

Dusty   Wills. Dusty Wills.

Raeburn   Nice to meet you, Dusty . . . Wait, *the* Dusty Wills . . . as in the notorious thief, Dusty Wills?

Dusty   The one and only.

Raeburn   Mark my words, Detective, if anything else goes missing, I'll have your head for this. My painting is a national treasure. Not that I expect the pair of you to understand.

Pidcock   Oh, *El Arte del Engaño, The Art of Deception* by Christiano De La Main, his last painting before his death in 1772. Quite an exceptional piece.

Dusty *gives* **Pidcock** *a look.*

Raeburn   Yes, you know your art, Detective, I'm impressed. Tell me, are you quite artistic yourself?

Pidcock   I'm not as it happens, although it was always suspected as a child.

Raeburn   Good. (*Beat.*) Yes, quite, well, it's only right for it to be returned to Raeburn Manor, to be with its rightful owner.

Pidcock   Don't worry, my lord, we'll get it back.

Penelope *enters.*

Penelope   Oh, hello everyone, I didn't think you would all still be here. Honey, may I remind you that this is my daily private hour.

Raeburn   But there's an investigation, my dear.

Penelope   But this is my private hour.

Raeburn   Well, I want to find my painting.

Penelope   Well, I want you to leave.

Raeburn   Fine! It's just a priceless painting after all . . . Wouldn't want you to be unsatisfied, would we?

Penelope   Well, it wouldn't be for the first time!

They aggressively laugh in each others face.

Raeburn   Gentlemen, if you would kindly follow me, we can resume this elsewhere.

Dusty   Just a second, old chap. Lady Raeburn, what exactly is this private hour?

Penelope   Well, it's private.

Dusty   My dear, a priceless painting has been stolen and we're here to find the culprit.

Pidcock   Please, Dustin, leave this to the professionals . . . a priceless painting has been stolen and we're here to find the culprit.

Dusty   If you take a daily private hour at the same time, that would mean you were missing without an alibi right before the painting / was declared stolen.

Pidcock   / was declared stolen. Yes.

Penelope   It's time on my own when I can call acquaintances or make business calls. In fact, I'm expecting a call very soon and I'd like you to leave.

Dusty/Pidcock   Business calls to an art dealer perhaps?

Telephone rings.

In fact, this could be him right now!

They both rush over to the telephone and tussle to answer it

Penelope   No no /

Pidcock *picks up the phone.*

Pidcock   Hello? Excuse me?! You've got what for Lady Raeburn?

Penelope   I can explain.

Pidcock   Oh, you must be the delivery man.

Raeburn   Delivery man? We aren't expecting any deliveries?

Pidcock   He says he needs to unload his goods.

Raeburn   Is it a large delivery?

Pidcock   Is it a big one? . . . (*To* **Lord Raeburn**.) He said he's had no complaints.

Raeburn   Well tell him we'll send some maids to help.

Pidcock   How about we send some maids to join as well . . . Yes . . . That's right, well that's good to hear. (*To* **Lord Raeburn**.) He said it's what he's always dreamed of.

Raeburn   Excellent, well we'll meet him at the rear of the house.

Pidcock   They'll be taking you in at the back passage . . . (*Pulls phone away.*) He seems very pleased with that . . .

Raeburn   And when shall we be expecting him?

Pidcock   When will you be coming? . . . Oh. (*To* **Lord Raeburn**.) He already has.

Raeburn   Outstanding! See that, Detective, that, that is the efficiency we need around here, isn't that right, dear?

Penelope (*extremely uncomfortable*)   Yes, quite. Well, if you'll excuse me, I think I'll have a lie down.

Penelope *exits.*

Pidcock   Now, the painting must have been stolen earlier that afternoon before spectators arrived. But how would someone be able to gain access to the manor?

Raeburn   Well, there is only one entrance into the estate which leads directly to the main doors, but you can also access the manor from the rear exit around the back.

Dusty   The thief could have slipped out back with the painting without being unnoticed.

Raeburn   The suspect would still have to leave the estate from the front and no one goes unnoticed.

Pidcock   And how do we exit from the rear?

Raeburn   You would have to go through the kitchen.

Pidcock   The kitchen, good, let's start there.

Dusty   Yes, Detective, let's. So, who was in the kitchen on the day in question?

Raeburn   That would be our new cook, Bertha. She made an incredible beef tartare for the auction.

Pidcock   A beef what?

Raeburn   Tartare.

Pidcock   Ta-ta! But before you leave, could you tell us a bit more about Bertha?

Raeburn   Well, she is quite the timid type but a remarkable cook. Did you know that she trained at Il Ristorante Scadente?

Pidcock   Sounds exotic.

Raeburn   Oh Detective, you don't get more exotic than Bertha, such a delicate, gentle being.

Pidcock (*shmoozing*)   Well, she sounds like just my type.

Raeburn   Well, you are a man of the finer things after all, are you not? She is a culinary genius who can do some incredible things with her hands.

Pidcock   Say no more. Please, may we speak with her?

Raeburn   Very well, I will get Nora to release Bertha. I think you two will hit it off just fine.

Lord Raeburn *exits.*

Scene Five

Dusty   Release? Detective, I don't have a good feeling about this.

Pidcock   Oh really, and why is that?

Dusty   Well, I just think we need to be cautious about Bertha. Just like in any great detective novel, the criminal is always the first person you meet.

Pidcock   Oh, you're just worried she won't find you charming . . . Frank.

Dusty   I'm not worried, Detective.

Pidcock   I can sense it a mile off.

Dusty   Oh is that so?

Pidcock   Now you keep out of this and let me do the talking. I've met people like Bertha before . . .

Bertha *enters.*

Bertha *is a large, intimidating presence with a stern face which would put shivers down the bravest people's spines. Her accent is strong with a deep, bellowing voice. Her apron is filthy and covered in blood. She slowly creeps on stage.*

Pidcock   . . . They're weak and feeble, she'll be like putty in my hands. So this would be a good opportunity for you to watch the professional and maybe take some notes.

Dusty   But Detective . . .

Pidcock   You just keep your mouth shut and listen, we will have her quivering in her boots in no time.

Dusty   But Detective . . .

Pidcock   I can sense you're nervous, Dustin, it's understandable but she'll be a pushover, so don't be so intimidated.

Bertha   Hello!

Pidcock *turns around and screams. Lights flicker and thunder sounds.*

Bertha   Ey up, cocka! How's tha bin?

Pidcock*'s eyes light up as he hasn't got a clue what she is saying.*

Dusty   Remember, Pidcock, don't be so intimidated.

Pidcock *gulps.*

Pidcock   Hello, I'm Detective Pid – AHH.

Bertha *shakes* **Pidcock***'s hand too tight.*

Pidcock   Pidcock . . . and this is Dustin Wills.

Bertha *shakes* **Dusty***'s hand.* **Dusty** *notices her bracelet, however she releases it and tries to hide her wrist.*

Bertha   I'm Bertha, the cook.

Pidcock   And what is it you do?

Bertha   Cook.

Pidcock *gulps.*

Pidcock   And what were you doing in the kitchen on the day of the auction?

Bertha   Cooking. Partner's not very bright, is he, shagger?

Bertha *laughs manically. The lights begin to flicker, thunder sounds, followed by* **Pidcock** *and* **Dusty** *laughing hesitantly.*

Dusty   Now my dear . . . I'm sure you are aware of us being here, we were wondering if you saw anything out of the ordinary on the day of the auction?

Bertha   Did I 'eckkers like, worked till noon and never left kitchen.

They look at each other in bewilderment.

Pidcock   I see, and no one was acting suspicious around the kitchen on the day of the auction?

Bertha   What tha tryin t' say 'bout my kitchen?

Lights flicker and thunder sounds.

Pidcock   I'm sorry, nothing, we are just trying to piece things together, that's all.

Bertha   Eee by gum! I told ya . . . I were working! I get a lot of people comin' int' my kitchen, I'm very approachable me
. . .

Thunder sounds and lights flicker again.

Pidcock   Yes, of course you are, Bertha.

Dusty   But do you know . . . might know . . . possibly know of anyone who might want to steal the painting?

Bertha   Were it expensive?

Pidcock   Very.

Bertha   Well then, everyone. They don't pay reyt well here.

Pidcock   Maybe that's why someone would steal it.

Bertha   I'm no thief, so a'd be careful what tha says aroun meh.

Pidcock   Yes, of course, you're quite right, thank you for your time, Bertha. Meanwhile, if you think of anyone who could be a suspect then please let us know.

Bertha *begins to exit then halts and turns around abruptly.* **Pidcock** *gets startled.*

Bertha *leaves.*

Pidcock   Well, that went a lot better than I imagined. I told you, Dustin, leave it to the professionals. She was a quivering wreck by the end of it.

Dusty   Was she?

Pidcock   Oh yes, Dustin. See, that's how you handle a case, with bravery and composure. Now it seems to be getting a little warm in here so I think I'll open the windows for some fresh air.

Pidcock *pulls back the curtains to reveal* **Bertha** *standing there. Lights flicker and thunder sounds. He screams and jolts back.*

Bertha   Av bin thinkin, if a were you, ad chat t' gardeners.

Pidcock   Who?

She squares up to **Pidcock**.

No please, I'm sorry, I don't know what you said.

Bertha   T' gardeners.

Dusty   Gardeners.

Bertha   T' gardeners.

Pidcock   Ahhh, gardeners!

Bertha   Aye, gardeners! Mick and Roy, reyt dodgy, I sawwa one of them gardeners leavin' grounds before auction, might ov ad painting for all a know, and t' other one has always bin sniffing round parts he shunt, in people's bedrooms n ladies' drawers.

Pidcock   Thank you! Well, if you could send them in, that would be great.

Bertha *begins to exit then halts and turns around abruptly.* **Pidcock** *gets startled.*

Bertha *exits.*

Dusty   Bravery and composure . . . I've made a note of it.

Pidcock   Please, I knew she was there the entire time. It's all part of my master plan. Now, I really need to leave to get some fresh air.

Pidcock *opens the front door to reveal* **Bertha** *standing behind it. The lights flicker and thunder sounds.* **Pidcock** *screams louder.*

Bertha   And I'll tell you this for free . . . Hear all, see all, say nowt. Eat all, sup all, pay nowt. And if ever tha does owt for nowt – Allus do it fer thissen . . . Does tha understand?

Pidcock *nods and shakes his head slowly.*

Pidcock   Yes? Well . . . That will be all, thank you, Bertha, you've been . . . Yes. Thank you.

Dusty   Yes, thank you, Bertha. It has been a pleasure to have you with us.

Bertha   Ta-ra love, I got a cob in the oven so I best be off.

Pidcock (*laughs*)   Oh? Yes and the same to you.

Bertha *begins to exit then halts and turns around abruptly.* **Pidcock** *gets startled, his scream is almost silent and he begins to hide.*

Bertha *exits.*

Dusty   I must say it's a privilege to watch you investigate and I am very excited to hear what you discovered from that insightful display of interrogating.

Pidcock   I know what you're thinking and yes, it wasn't easy. I realise English isn't her first language but my impeccable hearing was able to detect a vital clue which may bring us one step closer to solving the mystery.

Dusty   Oh, and what is that?

Pidcock   I detected that Bertha is in fact . . . the cook.

Dusty   Well, aren't you an investigative genius.

Pidcock   Oh and you think you can do better? Please enlighten me on anything I may have missed.

Dusty   Well, didn't you notice that smell?

Pidcock   I apologise, I was very nervous.

Dusty   No, not you, her.

Pidcock   I thought she smelled rather pleasant.

Dusty   Exactly, she was wearing perfume.

Pidcock   What kind of cook wears perfume?

Dusty   That's my point, and not to mention her jewellery.

Pidcock   What jewellery?

Dusty   Her bracelet, why would she wear such an expensive item whilst working in a kitchen. Very unusual for someone on a cook's wages to possess, especially when she said they don't pay well here.

Beat.

Pidcock   Ah yes, and she is also the cook.

Dusty   She also said that she saw one of the gardeners leaving the grounds on the day. Did she really see them or could it be a set up? Plus, how would she have seen them unless she was out of her kitchen. If she was, then why?

Pidcock   Good work, Dustin, I was wondering when you would discover that.

Scene Six

Mick, *a gardener, enters, shaking, old, hunched over, with a small beard and a walking stick.*

Mick   Good morning, officers.

Pidcock   Ermm, good morning? How can we help you?

Mick *bumps into things, the detectives help him.*

Mick   Well, it's more, how can I help you?

Pidcock   We're quite alright, thank you. We're conducting an investigation here.

Mick   Ahh, I see.

Pidcock   Do you?! Well, if you don't mind, could you kindly move along; we are here to question people.

Mick   Don't you want to question me?

Dusty   No thank you, sir.

Mick (*to Dusty*)   It's not every day I get to speak to a lovely young lady like yourself.

Dusty   How could he be of use, his eyesight is terrible?

Mick   Cor blimey, governor. Please forgive my appearance, I didn't know I was in the presence of a sophisticated gentleman like yourself.

Pidcock   Eyesight seems perfectly fine to me.

Dusty   We're actually waiting to speak to the gardeners.

Mick   I am the gardener.

Pidcock (*scoffs*)   You're a gardener?

Mick   That's right, been a family business for many years, passed down from father to son, from generation to generation.

Pidcock   Oh, a father and son business, well that explains it. Sorry sir, perhaps we could speak to the son instead?

Mick   You're speaking to him.

Pidcock   Pardon?

Mick   I am the son. I work with my father . . .

Dusty   Wait, you don't mean to say . . .

Enter **Roy**, *even older, shaking heavily, with two walking sticks.*

Roy   They ain't sending me back if that's what you think.

Mick   No, Father, the detectives just want to ask a few questions.

Pidcock   How are you today, sir?

Roy   About 3 o'clock.

Mick   You might have to speak up, he's a bit deaf.

Roy   My hearing is fine, just like my other parts, they're all perfectly fine! . . . Nice to see you again, officer.

Pidcock   Please sit down, Mr . . .

Roy   Watt.

Pidcock   Sorry. What is your name?

Mick   That's right.

Pidcock   No, no, what is your name?

Roy   Watt is my name.

Pidcock   No point asking me.

Mick   I just told you.

Pidcock   Told me what?

Mick   My name.

Pidcock   Which is?

Roy   What?

Pidcock   Your name?!

Mick   Watt!

Pidcock   WHAT IS IT?!

Dusty   WATT!

Pidcock   Don't you start.

Dusty   No, no, Watt is his name.

Pidcock   I'm clearly trying to find that one out, Dustin!

Mick   I'm Mick and this is Roy.

Pidcock   Mick and Roy what?

Mick/Roy/Dusty   Yes.

Pidcock   AHHHHHHHHHHHHH. I'm beginning to lose my patience. Fine, if you want to remain anonymous, so be it. Roy, can you tell us where you were on the day of the auction.

Roy   No.

Pidcock   No? What do you mean, no?

Roy   Well, you see, my memory's not as sharp as it once was. And to make matters worse my . . . memory's not as sharp as it once was.

Dusty   Did you see anyone else in the great hall at the time?

Roy   I saw Bertha and stew.

Pidcock   Mmm stew, delicious! Are you sure you saw the cook?

Dusty   Because without an alibi you were the closest to the painting before it went missing.

Mick   We were in the great hall erecting a floral arrangement for the evening reception. Red Carnations. Did you know they are the national flower of Spain. Hola.

Roy   My boy is taking me on holiday to Spain, the beautiful Sunnyside Resort.

Mick   Now isn't the time, Father.

Dusty   For a place that supposedly doesn't pay well, a lot of the staff are living a life of luxury.

Pidcock   Mick, you say were arranging flowers throughout the day of the auction, but we have witnesses that saw one of you leaving the grounds just before the auction.

Mick   Oh, did I? I was, errr, out getting wood for the new garden fence. (*Whispers.*) You see, the last one was put up by my father here almost fifty years ago, it's seen better days.

Roy   I'm not that old, you cheeky sod.

Mick   I meant no offence, Father.

Roy   What?

Mick   I meant no offence, Father!

Roy   Oh . . . I thought you were building a fence.

Mick   There is a fence.

Roy   But you just said there was no fence.

Mick   I said no offence to your fence that I'm replacing with a new fence.

Roy   Whose fence?

Mick   My fence, I said, no offence.

Roy   Noah Fence, he ain't worked here in forty years, he isn't coming back, surely not?

Mick   Shirley Knott, what's she got to do with any of this? I said your fence is so old it's practically an antique.

Pidcock   Anna Teak, how the devil do you know her?

Dusty   ENOUGH! That will be all, you're free to go.

Mick   We're no thieves, we're hard-working men! We have our family's name to uphold.

Pidcock   Which is what?

Mick   That's right, Detective, and don't you forget it.

Pidcock *tenses in frustration.*

Dusty   Thank you for your time, gentlemen.

The gardeners exit.

Pidcock   So, the gardeners . . .

Dusty   There's more to them to uncover, I feel they may lead us further in this investigation.

Pidcock   Yes, I agree.

Dusty   Bertha did say she saw a gardener leave, which Mick unknowingly confessed, but why is he taking his father away? And where exactly?

Pidcock   And how, Dustin? We can't forget about the poor paying conditions they apparently have here.

Dusty   Which certainly gives them all a strong motive to steal a painting.

Pidcock   You're right, Dustin, we are starting to get somewhere.

Dusty   If only a clue would just appear unexpectedly.

Pidcock   Oh, that simple, huh?

Dusty   It happens in all the great detective novels, a clue will always reveal itself.

Pidcock   Oh, please, what do you think is going to happen? A clue will fall at your feet.

Dusty *opens a book from which a small book falls out.*

Dusty   I found a clue!

Pidcock   Beginner's luck! What is it?

Dusty   It's a small notebook, but all of the pages are blank, except for one.

Pidcock   What's on it?

Dusty   It's a number, with the initials 'D. W.'.

Pidcock   Dustin Wills! I knew you were involved in this. Well, you're coming with me. This was easy, you've been caught, case closed, you're still a crook. I knew it!

Dusty   Dash it all, why would I have something to do with this? I was on the inside when the painting was stolen, don't forget. Initials inside of a book which coincidentally correspond with mine isn't exactly something to conclude an entire investigation is it, Detective?

Pidcock (*pondering*)   Hmmm, maybe you're right, but I have my doubts about you. I'll keep hold of that if you don't mind. I don't want you tampering with the evidence.

Dusty   So be it, but let it be on record, Detective . . . I found the first clue . . .

Pidcock (*mocking him*)   I found the first clue. Beginner's luck, I say! Finding a clue isn't like picking flowers, you can't just pluck one from the ground . . .

Pidcock *pulls out a bundled up garment from the flowers.*

Pidcock   I found a clue!

Dusty   I told you, old boy, it doesn't always have to be complicated.

Pidcock   What is it?

Dusty   You tell me.

They unfold a large pair of lady's underwear, both pinching it either side.

Pidcock   I've heard of early bloomers but that is ridiculous! (*To audience or* **Dusty***: 'Like you could do much better'.*)

Dusty   Well, it looks like you could say, we're finally getting to the bottom of things . . .

Pidcock   That's enough of that, Dustin. It's about time you started to take this more seriously!

Scene Seven

Nora *walks in with the tea tray and sees the underwear.*

Nora   Oh hello, Detectives.

Pidcock (*startled*)   Nora!

Pidcock *spins around still holding the garment giving the impression he is wearing lingerie.*

Nora   I brought you some . . . oh my, I'm sorry for interrupting, again.

Pidcock   No, Nora, it's not what it looks like.

Nora   It's none of my business what you two get up to. As long as you're happy, I'm happy.

Dusty   Nora, may we have a few minutes of your precious time?

Nora   Is there anything you'd like?

Pidcock   Just a few matters we'd like to discuss with you.

Nora   Oh, ermm, if I must.

Nora *looks uneasy.*

Dusty   There's nothing to be nervous about, my sweet.

Nora Nervous? I'm not nervous. What makes you think I'm nervous?

Nora *brings the tea over to them, shaking.*

Pidcock Oh please, allow me.

Pidcock *takes the tea, then he begins to shake before* **Dusty** *takes the cup and saucer and places them down on the table.*

Dusty We just need to ask you a few questions about the stolen painting.

Nora Oh Detective, you don't think little old me stole the painting?

Dusty Of course not, my dear, we just want to know if you saw anything unusual on the day of the auction.

Nora Oh of course, there was something in particular about the lord asking for tea and coffee to be brought up to his room.

Pidcock And what is unusual about that?

Nora He never drinks coffee, and neither does Lady Raeburn.

Dusty Perhaps they wanted a change? You can't blame them wanting something strong and rich, do you, Nora?

Dusty *begins to pose.*

Pidcock You never stop, do you?!

Nora Oh my, well Dusty, that may be, but neither of them share a bedroom and they haven't for some time. Oh, I am constantly running back and forth between the lord and lady and I've had enough.

I'm sorry I look dishevelled but I've been working here as the head maid ever since I was twenty-one.

Pidcock Nonsense, you look great for a woman of your age.

Nora (*cries*) Ahh, I'm twenty-two.

Dusty   Detective, may I talk to you in private?

They move away from **Nora**.

Dusty   I really think we should try and charm her, get her on our side. After all, maids are notorious for listening in on people's private conversations.

Nora   That's not true.

Dusty *and* **Pidcock** *look at* **Nora**, *then back to each other.*

Pidcock   Fine.

They turn to **Nora**, *compose themselves and, like peacocks, begin to walk towards her, walking as if they were modelling the latest fashion.* **Dusty** *leads the way, his voice is smooth, seductive.* **Pidcock** *tries to follow suit, however his body is robotic and uncomfortable and his voice changes completely as he attempts to copy* **Dusty**.

Dusty   Dear sweet Nora, beautiful Nora, will you tell us what caused the friction between the lord and lady, please.

Nora   Oh, anything for you, Dusty. Well, Lady Raeburn never wanted to marry Lord Raeburn, but she refused every suitor and was left with no other choice.

Pidcock (*flirting terribly*)   And why, pray tell, did she refuse every suitor?

Nora   Oh, ermmm that's not really my place to say, I am afraid . . .

Dusty   But my darling, why was Lady Raeburn so against marriage? We all deserve love after all.

Nora   Oh, you're quite right . . . well, rumour has it that she had a sweetheart but he was denied her hand as he was a working boy.

Pidcock   Is that so? And what happened to Lady Raeburn?

Nora   That's none of my business or yours, Detective, and I think I must leave.

Pidcock   Oh, not yet.

Pidcock *grabs* **Nora***'s tray, refusing her exit.*

Dusty   Remember, Detective, charm her.

Pidcock   I am charming her!

Pidcock *begins to look more possessed than flirtatious.*

Pidcock   Nora! We still need to know about the lord and lady's relationship?

Nora   I'm sorry but it's private, you won't get a word out of me.

Dusty   Detective, gentle.

Pidcock   But honey cheeks, we need to know for the investigation.

Nora   Well I don't care.

Pidcock   Well I do.

Nora   Give me the tray.

Pidcock   Fine.

Pidcock *releases the tray which hits* **Nora** *directly on the head, knocking her back to a chair.*

Nora   When the lady's parents found out she loved a working boy, they were furious and sent her to the countryside for a few months . . .

Pidcock (*amazed*)   It worked.

Nora   Sorry, I don't know what got into me.

Dusty   What can be so bad that she was sent off like that?

Pidcock   Nora, could you tell us more about how Lord Raeburn comes into this?

Nora   I'm sorry, Detective, I have a job to protect at the end of the day and I am feeling rather woozy.

Dusty   I understand, she's right, Detective. Thank you, Nora, you should get some rest now. You've been very helpful. Give me that tray, Pidcock.

Dusty *goes to grab the tray off* **Pidcock**, *however* **Pidcock** *refuses.*

Pidcock   Dustin, we're not finished, let go.

Dusty   Leave the poor girl alone, you've done enough damage.

Pidcock   We've only just started.

Dusty   We can wait.

Pidcock   I can't.

Dusty   Let go!

Pidcock   Dustin . . .!

They struggle with the tray until it is swung round and hits **Nora**, *again.*

Nora   Lord Raeburn's past and family remain a mystery. When Penelope returned from the countryside almost a year later, he offered to save her family's reputation in exchange for the lady's hand in marriage and to become heir to the estate.

Dusty   Wait a minute, so you're telling me that this isn't Lord Henry's home?

Pidcock   So all of this is in fact Lady Raeburn's?

Nora (*gasps*)   Who told you that?

Dusty   So, Penelope is the rightful owner of the estate? But why is it Raeburn Manor?

Nora   I don't know what you're talking about, I haven't said anything. Now I really must go. Lord Raeburn will be looking for me and I don't want to upset him.

Dusty   Yes, I think she is right, we'd better let her go, Pidcock. Give me the tray.

Pidcock Fine!

Pidcock *lets go of the tray which causes* **Dusty** *to spin around and hit* **Nora** *straight in the head.*

Pidcock I say, look what you've done.

Dusty Me?

Nora He's not Lord Raeburn at all, he's . . . he's . . .

Dusty He's what Nora? He's what?

Nora *falls unconscious.*

Dusty *gives* **Pidcock** *a look.*

Dusty Quick, Pidcock, let's get her to the window, get her some fresh air.

The pair lift **Nora** *and carry her over to the window.* **Pidcock** *struggles to lift the window.*

Dusty Open the window, Pidcock.

Pidcock I'm trying but it's stuck!

Roy *the gardener enters, throughout the scene he grows more and more concerned with what is being suggested.*

Dusty Come on, Pidcock, we haven't got time.

Pidcock I'm giving it everything I've got.

Dusty Hurry, Pidcock, Nora needs this.

Pidcock I can't get it up.

Dusty Do you need a hand?

The window opens slightly.

Pidcock No, that's alright, I think it's nearly there.

Dusty Give it a good yank.

Pidcock I am yanking at it.

Dusty Quickly, Pidcock.

Pidcock   Wait, something is happening.

Pidcock *lifts the window.*

Pidcock   AHH, I've got it up!

Dusty   Bravo, old chap. Quick, get her in position.

Pidcock   I thought I was going to ask one of the gardeners to give me a hand.

Roy   MR RAEBURN!

Roy *exits.*

Dusty *and* **Pidcock** *get a fright and turn around sharply.*

Nora *falls out of the window.*

The pair turn back around and are bewildered as to where **Nora** *may have gone. Suddenly it clicks.*

Dusty/Pidcock   Nora!

Nora *flings herself over the windowsill, she looks dishevelled with twigs and leaves in her hair.*

Dusty   Here, Nora, let me help you.

Pidcock   Allow me, Nora, we can't let a beast like him near you.

Dusty   It was your fault she's like this. Pull her up.

Pidcock   Don't worry, Nora, you're in perfectly safe hands.

Pidcock *taps the wall, suddenly the window drops on* **Nora,** *trapping her.* **Pidcock** *and* **Dusty** *are both in complete shock and frantically try to see how they can make this situation better.*

Dusty   Oh no, not again, Nora!

Pidcock *tries to open the window but it's jammed again. They heave and pull* **Nora** *and the window but it won't budge.* **Nora***'s arms flail around, ragdoll-like.*

Pidcock   The window is stuck again.

Dusty   Nora, we're going to get you out of this.

Suddenly the door opens.

Pidcock   Quick, Dustin, someone's coming!

Dusty *closes the curtains hiding* **Nora**.

Enter **Lord Raeburn.**

Pidcock   Ah, Lord Raeburn, what are you doing here?

Raeburn   This is my home, you imbecile. Now do either of you care to explain why I have a very distressed gardener who is claiming something very peculiar is happening in here?

Pidcock   It's really not what it looks like!

Raeburn   Really? Do I look like a fool to you?

Pidcock   Certainly not, my lord.

Raeburn   Because to me it looks like you two were snooping around my reception room. Nothing gets past me.

Pidcock   That is completely correct. Oh, it looks like you caught us in the act.

Dusty (*bewildered*)   Yes, *we* were just searching for possible clues.

Dusty *and* **Pidcock** *begin examining the room.* **Dusty** *makes his way to the chest of drawers but it's locked.*

Raeburn   Well, I understand you have a job to do, Detective, but please don't touch everything.

Dusty   The drawer appears to be locked, any particular reason?

Raeburn   Yes, and I'd appreciate it if you didn't try to force it open, you brute, it's an antique after all and the key has been missing for some years now. I'm glad I caught you, before you did any more damage.

Nora *groans from behind the curtain.*

Raeburn   Did you say something?

Pidcock (*imitating* **Nora**'s *groan*)   Ooohhhh, no no no, we wouldn't dream of damaging your beautiful home.

Raeburn   Yes, you're right, it is beautiful and very expensive.

Nora *groans from behind the curtain.*

Raeburn   What was that?

Dusty (*imitating* **Nora**'s *groan*)   Ooohhhh, and do tell me who this handsome chap is right here.

Dusty *points the attention away to a large painted portrait resembling* **Lord Raeburn**, *however the plaque is missing.*

Raeburn   That is a portrait of my great grandfather, he was a noble count, you know?

Pidcock   That's funny, Lady Raeburn said you were a bit of a count yourself . . .

Dusty   His name appears to be missing?

Raeburn (*uncomfortable*)   Oh yes, that is a shame, his plaque seems to have been misplaced, like everything else round here. But enough of that, if you are to snoop around here, do it delicately and away from that drawer in particular.

Nora *groans from behind the curtain.*

Pidcock   Ooh. Yes, my Lord.

Raeburn   Yes, well, I'll be off now. Good day, gentlemen.

Dusty/Pidcock   Good day, my lord.

Lord Raeburn *exits.*

Dusty   Quick, Pidcock!

They pull the curtain back revealing a very cross and dazed **Nora**.

Dusty   Oh my. There you are, my darling, looking as beautiful as ever, please allow us to help.

They manage to lift the window and help **Nora** *onto her feet.*

Pidcock   Yes, that's better. Perhaps you'd like a nice comfy seat. Perhaps you could tell us who Lord Raeburn really is.

Nora   He is my employer and he will be very cross at the pair of you!

Nora *tries to exit.*

Dusty   No, Nora, please stay.

Nora   Get your hands off me.

Nora *shrugs them off and heads towards the SR door.*

Pidcock   Don't let her leave! Nora, who is Lord Raeburn?

Dusty   Please, Nora, come back.

Nora   Never, I am leaving and you can't stop me! You just wait until I tell the lord about you two.

Lord Raeburn *enters the room again, hitting* **Nora** *with the door.*

Raeburn   I almost forgot to say, if either of you two see Nora, tell her I'd like a word with her.

Dusty/Pidcock   Certainly, my lord.

They both shake their heads. **Lord Raeburn** *exits revealing a dazed* **Nora** *behind the door.*

Pidcock   Nora, allow us to help.

Dusty   Yes, please take a seat.

Pidcock   Allow me to get you a drink, Nora.

Pidcock *looks around the room and finds the decanter, he pours a drink and hands it to* **Nora**.

Dusty   There, there, Nora, just relax here. That's nice, isn't it? The detective will get you a nice drink of . . . Whiskey? . . . Really?

Pidcock   That's all I could find!

Dusty   Now, Nora, I believe you have a little secret to tell us, don't you?

Nora   I heard the detective crying in the toilets earlier.

Pidcock   Must be another detective. Please drink up, Nora.

Dusty   Now, Nora, you were saying that Lord Raeburn wasn't exactly who he says he is, can you elaborate?

Pidcock   Who is he really?

Nora   Wy . . . Wy . . .

Pidcock   Why? Because we need to know!

Pidcock *feeds* **Nora** *the glass of whiskey.* **Nora** *is in and out of consciousness.*

Nora   More . . . More . . .

Pidcock   Fine, if you insist on having more.

They feed the whiskey to her again as she tries to refuse until suddenly she is unconscious again. The pair stand back and look at each other in a panic, is she dead?

Pidcock   Nora? Nora? . . .

Dusty   Good heavens.

Pidcock   Oh dear.

Dusty   Oh dear, oh dear.

Lord Raeburn *enters.*

The pair turn to him.

Dusty/Pidcock   Oh dear, oh dear, oh dear.

Raeburn   My goodness, what is the meaning of this?

Pidcock   My lord, it's not what it looks like, honest.

Dusty   It's really not.

Raeburn   No? Because it looks to me like the maid has helped herself to my good whiskey and rendered herself unconscious.

Pidcock   My goodness, that's exactly what has happened.

Pidcock *gives* **Dusty** *a look.*

Raeburn   I thought this would be a straightforward investigation but ever since you two have gotten involved the place is in utter chaos.

Pidcock   I can only apologise, my lord.

Raeburn   I'm afraid that's not good enough, you need to interrogate more suspects and find my precious painting.

Pidcock   You're quite right, sir.

Dusty   Yes, we should definitely interrogate more suspects. So, why did you host an auction if you intended to steal the painting?

Raeburn   I . . . beg your pardon?

Pidcock   Sorry about him, my lord!

Dusty   A stolen painting would be worth a lot more on the black market, so maybe that's why you wanted to make it appear stolen, so you could reap both the rewards!

Raeburn   I don't need the hassle or the money! And I certainly don't need to be accused by a thief like you!

I want this painting found and intact, do you understand? No more funny business.

Pidcock   Of course, my lord.

Lord Raeburn *exits.*

Scene Eight

Pidcock   I swear to god if you ever undermine me like that again . . .

Dusty   Are you threatening me, Detective?

Pidcock   From now on, there will be no more disrespectful comments about me or the lord of this establishment.

Dusty   Why do you defend him, pray tell? You don't even like Lord Raeburn.

Pidcock   And why do you presume you know me so well?

Dusty   I'm the master of reading people. I could deduce you easily.

Pidcock   Ha, clearly you have read wrong, for I am a heterosexual.

Dusty   What?

Pidcock   Your powers of seduction will not work on me.

Dusty   I said deduce you, not seduce you.

Pidcock   Very well . . . Deduce this.

Pidcock *pounces on* **Dusty** *and they begin to tussle, one of them grabs* **Nora***'s tray.*

Scene Nine

Nora   Sorry, I must have dozed off!

Nora *wakes to see them with the tray which triggers a flashback causing her to scream.*

Pidcock   No no, Nora, it's not what you think.

Nora   No! Stay back, I'm warning you.

Pidcock   No no, Nora, it's not what you think.

Dusty   Please, Nora, we just want to talk to you. I'm afraid we're at a loss, you see.

Pidcock   You're the only one who is cooperating.

Nora   Yes, I have the headache to prove it.

Dusty   We are sorry, Nora, if there is anything we can do to make it up to you, please let us know . . .

Nora *ponders for a moment.*

Nora   Hmmm, well there is one thing . . . if you really meant it.

Pidcock   What?

Dusty   Anything.

Nora   You see, all I ever wanted in life was two loving parents.

Pidcock   Didn't you know your parents?

Nora   Sadly not, I was raised in an orphanage. That's where I met Lady Raeburn, she used to frequently visit the orphanage and took an instant liking to me. So much so, she even brought me to Raeburn Manor to work and get an education.

Dusty   You were an orphan?

Nora   Yes, that's right.

Dusty   I'm sorry to hear about that, Nora.

Nora   When I was an orphan I always used to have a dream of sitting by the radio listening to music whilst watching a couple who were madly in love with each other, just dancing away in each other's arms . . .

Pidcock   What a lovely image.

Nora   A loving couple . . . like yourselves.

The penny drops for the pair of them, they look at each other in horror.

Dusty/Pidcock   Oh no, Nora, we aren't /

Nora   Dance for me. Dance for that poor orphan girl I once was.

*During this, **Dusty** and **Pidcock** desperately try to convince **Nora** that they aren't willing to dance or entertain the idea.*

Dusty/Pidcock   We aren't . . . we don't dance . . . two left feet . . . you don't want to see that . . .

Nora   Oh very well, that is a shame.

Pidcock   Apologies, Nora, we are disappointed in ourselves for seeing you so upset.

Nora   Yes, yes. I understand . . . You know who will be disappointed that I'm upset? . . . My good friend Bertha.

Dusty/Pidcock   Bertha?!

Nora   I would hate to see how she would react when she hears about our previous encounter.

Dusty   Come, Nora, is there anything else we can do?

Nora   No, just dance.

Dusty/Pidcock   But, Nora.

Nora   Just do it.

Dusty/Pidcock   But . . . but . . .

Nora   BERTHA!!!

Pidcock *and* **Dusty** *snap together in a slow dance style dance move, slowly and painfully moving around the space.* **Nora** *plays music from the radio.*

Nora   Oh, that is just beautiful.

Pidcock   I hope you're happy, Nora.

Nora   I am, now look at each other . . . and tell them how much they mean to you.

They exchange a look.

Dusty   I, ermmmm . . . I don't really want to . . .

Nora   Oh Bertha.

There is a lot of hesitancy.

Dusty   You . . . You . . . mean the world to me, Detective . . .

Pidcock   Really?

Dusty   No, you idiot.

Dusty *slaps* **Pidcock** *across the head.*

Nora   Now you, Detective . . .

Pidcock   I think we really got off on the wrong foot.

Pidock *stamps on* **Dusty's** *foot.*

Dusty   I can't tell you how much of an impact you have made in my life.

Dusty *returns with a punch to the stomach to* **Pidcock**.

Pidcock   You don't know how much I *need* you, Dustin.

Pidcock *returns with a knee to the stomach to* **Dusty**.

Dusty *tackles* **Pidcock** *to the chair and begins to choke him.*

Dusty   I always want to take your breath away.

Pidcock *swipes* **Dusty's** *leg so he's sitting on his lap.*

Pidcock   I just love to sweep you off your feet.

Nora *turns around and sees* **Dusty** *on* **Pidcock's** *lap.*

Nora   Oh, look at yourselves, you just can't take your hands off one another.

Pidcock/Dusty (*whilst being strangled*)   You can say that again!

Pidcock   You are the apple of my eye.

He pokes **Dusty** *in the eye which forces him off* **Pidcock**.

Nora   Oh, isn't that just wonderful, thank you for that, it brought a tear to my eye.

Dusty   And most definitely to mine, Nora.

Nora   Oh, I will certainly remember this for a long time.

Pidcock   I think it's safe to say we all will, Nora.

Dusty *makes a break for the radio to turn it off.*

Nora   I know a good relationship when I see one.

Pidcock   Yes, I'm sure you do, Nora. Speaking of relationships, Lady Raeburn could be in a lot of trouble unless you tell us who could also be a suspect in this case . . .

Nora   Well, there is Richard Wymore and his wife Mary.

Dusty   And who are they?

Nora   Well, Mary is an old friend of Lady Raeburn, although I have never heard them say a nice word about each other. Lady Raeburn often dreads her visiting, as she always ends up giving her money, god knows what for.

Dusty   And how did Lord Raeburn and Mr Wymore meet?

Nora   They seem to go way back as I often hear them reminisce about the past. Mr Wymore has a keen interest in artwork and in antiques, why, he even gifted Lord Raeburn that table!

Pidcock   Well, that would explain why Lord Raeburn is very protective over it.

Nora   Ohhh yes, very, no one is allowed to go in there. He won't even give Lady Raeburn the spare key!

Dusty   There's a key?

Nora   Yes, but Lord Raeburn keeps it hidden at all times.

Pidcock *and* **Dusty** *exchange a look to each other.*

Pidcock   I see, and on the day of the auction, did you happen to see either of them?

Nora   Hmm, not really, I did see Mr Wymore and Bertha together that afternoon. I mean, who ever heard of the help befriending a guest, I tell you.

Pidcock   Thank you, Nora, you've been most helpful. If you could send for them on your way that would be lovely.

Nora   I should warn you though, the Wymores are quite an unusual couple, so be careful.

Dusty   Thank you, Nora.

Nora *begins to exit.*

Nora   Oh, and of course, you are not permitted access to that drawer.

They halt.

Pidcock   Of course, Nora.

Nora *exits.*

Dusty   Pidcock, we need to get into that drawer!

Pidcock   Of course, Nora.

They creep towards it slowly.

Scene Ten

Enter **Richard Wymore**, *well to do, pompous and eccentric.*

Richard   Good afternoon, gentlemen. I was informed you'd like a word with me?

Pidcock *and* **Dusty** *are startled as if they have been caught in the act.*

Pidcock   Yes, hello, you must be Mr Wymore?

Richard   Richard Wymore or Dickie for short, at your service.

Pidcock   Mr Wymore, where were you on the day of the auction?

Richard   I wasn't around on the build up to the auction. Mary, my wife, was being, well, Mary. She was feeling a little flustered and wanted to stay in her room.

Dusty   What could have gotten her so worked up?

Richard   She had jewellery that went missing but she claims they were stolen.

Pidcock   Another theft. There appears to be a theme here. What is your profession, Mr Wymore?

Richard   I work in insurance.

Pidcock   Well, luckily with you working in insurance then, I presume all the jewellery was covered?

Richard   That would be fortunate, if so.

Dusty   And did you cover the painting?

Richard   I am afraid that is strictly confidential.

Dusty   Hmm, maybe we should have a talk with your wife, just to be safe.

Richard   That is an excellent idea, why not ask yourself, I'm sure she's just around the corner, let me find her, Mary . . . Mary?

Richard *exits.*

Pidcock   Seems we're dealing with more than one theft!

Dusty   I think you're right, Detective, but how come that was never reported to the police?

Pidcock   I don't know, Dustin, who do you think I am?

Dusty   The police?!

Pidcock   Oh yeah.

Dusty   And who comes all this way for a grand unveiling just to stay in their room?

Pidcock   Judging by the sound of her, I don't think I'd want to spend more than a few minutes alone with her.

Mary *enters. Dramatic, eccentric, bubbly and well to do.*

Mary   Hello, boys, forgive my intrusion but I just don't know who else to turn to.

Pidcock   Ahhh, Mrs Wymore, it is a pleasure to meet you.

Mary   Oh no, Detective, the pleasure is all mine.

Pidcock   May I say you smell delightful.

Mary   Do you like it, Detective? It's Oh De La.

Pidcock   It smells very familiar, maybe that's just how I imagine a famous movie actress would smell like.

Mary   Oh, Detective, what a charming man you are.

Pidcock   Thank you, Mrs Wymore, I get that a lot.

He fires a smug look towards **Dusty**.

Dusty   What is your relationship with Lady Raeburn?

Mary   We're like sisters.

Dusty   Is that why she gives you money?

Mary   Why she gives me money is no concern of yours, I have something of hers that she holds dearly, that's all.

Pidcock   Seems you're not revealing too much, Mrs Wymore.

Mary   Oh, Detective, that's because I'm not that easy.

Pidcock   Well, we may have to take our investigations further.

Mary   Oh, you read my mind. How about my place?

Pidcock   You are a sort.

Mary   Please excuse me while I freshen up . . . Byeee! (*Blows kiss.*)

Pidcock (*giggling and waving*)   Byeeeeee! (*Blows kiss.*)

Mary *exits.*

Pidcock   Looks like there's still some charm in the old snake after all.

Dusty   Detective, don't you find something unusual about that couple?

Pidcock   In what way?

Dusty   Could they be intersex, perhaps?

Pidcock   Aren't we all, Dustin? Mind your own business.

Dusty   What is Mary keeping safe for Penelope?

Pidcock   I too have many questions unanswered, Dustin, like what room number is she in for example?

Richard *enters.*

Richard   Nope, I am sorry, gentlemen, but I can't find her, did you have any luck yourselves?

Pidcock   You're never going to believe this, Mr Wymore, but you have just missed her, what are the chances.

Richard   Oh, that is a shame, but it happens often enough.

Pidcock   Aren't you and Mary close, Mr Wymore?

Richard   Close? Of course we're close, why you could say we are inseparable.

Dusty   You claim that you never left your room on the day of the auction, can you explain why you were seen being rather friendly to the cook that afternoon?

Richard   Oh, that's nothing unusual, I was merely thanking Bertha for making our favourite dessert to comfort us during the ordeal.

Dusty   Mr Wymore, can you tell us what Mary is keeping for Lady Raeburn, something sentimental perhaps?

Richard   I am afraid I can't answer that as I am none the wiser. I can't imagine Mary needing the money, what with her family's rich history. Perhaps you should ask my wife instead. Please, let me find her.

Richard *exits.*

Dusty   Detective, did you hear that? He said he's not close to Bertha.

Pidcock   Yes, I heard, Dustin, what's unusual about that?

Dusty   I never said her name, he already knew that.

Pidcock   My goodness, you're right, who addresses the help by their first name? It's almost as if they have already been acquainted.

Dusty   His wife Mary also comes from money. Didn't you notice the brooch on Mary's chest?

Pidcock   I couldn't stop staring at it /

Dusty   The brooch?

Pidcock   Ermm, yes . . . let's go with that . . .

Mary *enters.*

Mary   Cooeeee. Now, where were we, Detective?

They embrace.

I believe there was something I had to get off my chest . . .

Pidcock   I was thinking the same thing. Please, allow me to unburden you.

Dusty   Was this in reference to your stolen jewellery?

Pidcock *gives* **Dusty** *a look of disdain.*

Mary   Oh, my jewellery. Detective, you have to believe me, they were stolen, I am sure of it. Richard thinks I lost them but I swear I take good care of them, I do!

Pidcock   I am sure you do, just count your blessings that your husband has them covered.

Mary   Oh no, sadly he has never mentioned it. I am a lost cause, Detective.

She sobs. **Pidcock** *offers his support.*

Pidcock   Oh, come here my little rose bud.

They embrace.

Mary   Oh, Detective. I can't tell you how difficult it has been.

Pidcock   Now don't you fret no more.

Dusty   Excuse me, we are conducting an investigation here.

Mary   Oh, it's been so long since I've been held by a real man.

Pidcock   See that, Dustin? This is how a real man holds a woman.

Mary   Oh, Detective.

Pidcock   Call me Stuart.

Mary   Oh, Stuart!

Pidcock   Mary.

Dusty   Detective!

Pidcock   Dustin!

Mary   Richard!

Pidcock   Richard?

Richard *enters.*

Richard   Now, what exactly is going on here?

Pidcock   It's not what it looks like, I promise.

Dusty   The detective was showing me how a real man holds a woman.

Richard   What?!

Pidcock   That's not true. /

Dusty   It is true. /

Pidcock   I'm happily married. /

Dusty   No he's not.

Richard   Why, I oughta –!

Richard *raises a fist to* **Pidcock** *but* **Mary** *intervenes.*

Mary   Unhand him, Richard, you beast!

Mary *slaps his hand away*

Oh, why can't you let me be happy for once?!

Richard   Mary, please!

Mary   Leave me alone, Richard!

She exits sobbing. **Pidcock** *chases after her,* **Dusty** *goes to exit the stage.*

Pidcock   Oh Mary, wait for me! Please, let me comfort you.

Dusty   Just a second, Mr Wymore!

Richard *enters with* **Dusty** *SR.*

Richard   I did warn you about her, did I not? This is quite a common occurrence I'm afraid, and her mood swings are terrifying.

Richard *exits with* **Dusty** *SL.*

Mary *enters with* **Pidcock** *stage right.*

Mary   Oh, Detective, he just doesn't seem to care about me anymore, we used to be so close, practically joined at the hip.

Mary *exits with* **Pidcock** *stage left.*

Richard *enters with* **Dusty** *stage left.*

Richard   And you see that is why I had to get out of there, I just couldn't take it any longer. I've thought about calling it off many times in the past, believe me.

Richard *exits with* **Dusty** *SL.*

Mary *enters with* **Pidcock** *(US).*

Mary *cries hysterically.*

Pidcock   There, there, you don't have to worry about him for now, I am here.

Mary *exits with* **Pidcock** *(US).*

Richard *enters with* **Dusty** *SR walking backwards.*

Richard   Perhaps I was a little too hard on her, but sometimes she can be so insufferable. I mean, you saw the way she was just now.

Dusty *nods in agreement.*

Richard *exits with* **Dusty** *SR.*

Pidcock *enters holding a hand off stage.*

Pidcock   Ah, Mary, alone at last! Kiss me . . .

Mary *enters SL looking confused.*

Mary   Detective?

Pidcock *sees* **Mary** *at the other side of the room and is confused as to whose hand he is holding,* **Bertha** *enters holding* **Pidcock**'s *hand which causes him to scream, he tries to run but she grabs him and pulls him away SR.*

Mary *tries to run after him but is stopped by* **Richard**.

Richard   Mary, explain yourself!

Mary   Oh Richard, you are so two faced!

Richard   How dare you?

Mary   I want a man who completes me!

Pidcock *enters SR and* **Dusty** *enters SL.*

Pidcock   Ah, Mary, is everything alright?

Richard *turns sharply around.*

Richard   Actually, Detective, before you ruin another marriage, you will give me some time with my wife. Alone.

Pidcock   Certainly . . . we'll give you and your other half some privacy.

Pidcock *and* **Dusty** *exit.*

Richard   Mary, what is the meaning of this?

Mary   Oh really, Richard, you're not even half the man you once were!

Richard   How can you say such a thing?

Mary   Why is our love so difficult?

Richard   It would be easier if you were more respectable!

Mary   Oh, I will never be enough for you, Richard!

Richard   You're more than enough, Mary, and despite what you may think, I am still madly, madly in love with you . . . Kiss me . . .

He dips **Mary.**

Mary   Oh, Richard . . . Isn't this lovely? I could stay here for hours.

Richard   Come with me, Mary, we have some unfinished business to attend to.

Mary   Oh, Richard . . .

Richard   Mary!

Mary   Richard!

Richard   MARY!

They exit.

Interval.

Act Two

Scene One

Lights fade down.

Enter **Lord Raeburn**, *he switches on the radio, music plays, he reclines on a chair and begins to relax and falls asleep.*

Newsreporter (*on radio*)   We interrupt this broadcast to give you the latest news in the country. The Scouse Seductress is still at large, I repeat, the Scouse Seductress is still at large. Known for her incredible physique and raunchy ways, she entices her victims into a night of passion before stealing all their valuables. I sure hope she doesn't come to my house on twenty-four Clifftown Terrace on Duke Street to try and seduce me, that's for sure.

Soft music begins to play.

Enter **Pidcock** *and* **Dusty** (*SL*), *peeking out, making sure* **Lord Raeburn** *is asleep.*

They start to creep across the room to get the key, they hear a creak as they step on a floor board. They try again and again and still hear the same creak. **Pidcock** *lifts his knee and moves it back and forth, it creaks. He hits his leg and puts it back onto the floor, the creaking stops.*

They edge closer, **Pidock** *is about to sneeze,* **Dusty** *covers his nose with his finger and they both run over to the window, lift it up, but the sneeze has gone.*

They close the window and go past **Lord Raeburn**, *suddenly* **Pidcock** *sneezes,* **Lord Raeburn** *stirs and they start to rock the chair and hum 'Rock-a-bye Baby' to get him back off to sleep.*

Suddenly the radio switches and starts talking loudly. 'Have you had it with your radio having a mind of its own? Then it's time you switch to a TELEFUNKEN radio, it's TELEFUNKEN good, we know it's German engineering but they're desperately trying to get

*back into your good books. Head down to your local . . .' As the
radio plays* **Pidcock** *grabs it and heads over to the window where
he throws it out. The radio screams.*

Pidcock *and* **Dusty** *make their way to the locked drawer.* **Dusty**
mimes breaking into it. He gestures to **Pidcock** *to go and search for
something to break into the drawer with.* **Pidcock** *grabs the fire
poker; however, as he returns to* **Dusty**, **Lord Raeburn** *stirs
making* **Pidcock** *stab* **Dusty** *in the rear.* **Dusty** *yelps but covers his
mouth, he makes his way to the window, lifts it and screams out of
it. He storms across to* **Pidcock** *silently, grabbing hold of him and
dragging him over to the window where he steps on his foot, as he
yelps* **Dusty** *covers his mouth, and points* **Pidcock** *towards the
window where he lets out a huge scream.*

Dusty *makes his way back to the drawer and manages to pry it
open using his fingers. However,* **Pidcock** *falls into him, trapping*
Dusty's *fingers in the process. With* **Dusty**'s *fingers stuck and
nowhere to go, he grabs the nearby phone whilst simultaneously*
Pidcock *grabs the phone by the window SL and as* **Dusty** *screams
down the phone,* **Pidcock** *holds the receiver out of the window and
the scream can be heard going out.*

Dusty *gets his fingers out and* **Pidcock** *leans against the window
letting out a sigh of relief 'Phew!' Suddenly, the window slams shut
onto his hand and he can't lift it.* **Dusty** *runs over with a whiskey
decanter and hands it to* **Pidcock** *who screams into the glass
whiskey decanter before closing it and putting it back on the shelf
and making his way over to the drawer.*

As they get there, **Nora** *bursts through the door with the radio.*

Nora   You'll never guess what I found lying outside /

Before she finishes her sentence, **Pidcock** *covers* **Nora**'s *mouth as*
Dusty *takes the radio from her and places it on its perch. They pick
her up, take her over to the window and throw her out before
closing it and carrying on.*

They finally make their way to the drawer and open it, the pair celebrate together, joyously. **Dusty** *pulls out a plaque and examines it.*

If the audience applauds, the actors gesture to them to be quiet.

Pidcock   What's on it?

Dusty   Count Vymorov.

Pidcock   That's it?! (*He covers his mouth.*)

Suddenly **Lord Raeburn** *wakes up.*

Raeburn   My goodness! Gentlemen, what on earth are you doing in here? This is time for my afternoon nap and I am not to be disturbed!

Pidcock *and* **Dusty** *are startled. They hide the plaque behind* **Dusty**'*s back, they desperately want to leave.*

Pidcock   Apologies, my lord, we were just leaving.

Raeburn   No, no, since you insist on walking around as if you own the place, why not have a seat? Put your feet up! Why not help yourself to a drink?

Lord Raeburn *lifts the lid on the decanter and it lets out a huge scream with some choice words.* **Lord Raeburn** *puts the lid back on, startled.*

Raeburn   What the devil.

Pidcock   Oh, I would just ignore that sir, it's probably the drink talking. (*He laughs awkwardly.*) Let's go, Dusty.

Raeburn   Just a moment, have you had any more luck on tracking down the suspect?

Dusty   Not yet, Lord Raeburn, but we are close.

Raeburn   Oh, is that so? I have my suspicions about Nora, she is often lurking around and rarely cleans up after herself. I mean, look at this place. Have you had a chance to interrogate her yet?

Pidcock   Yes, we may have picked her brains once or twice.

Dusty   She was discussing how we all have our secrets, even the people you'd least suspect.

Lord Raeburn's *mannerism changes.*

Raeburn   Well, that does sound like Nora, she is forever fabricating fallacies, I would take no notice of her.

Penelope *enters.*

Penelope   Oh, there you are. You have been requested by Miss Anastasia Bramavich, apparently you had a meeting scheduled this afternoon and you missed it?

Raeburn   Oh bother, it must have slipped my mind.

Penelope   Even when the meetings have been a regular occurrence, scheduled for the same time everyday?

Raeburn   Yes, that is a funny one, what with everything going on, I feel I've lost my head.

Penelope   That's not the only thing you'll be losing if you carry on.

They laugh away then directly into each other's face.

Raeburn   Well, business waits for no man, duty calls and I answer. (*Excited.*) Hello business, is that you? I'm coming right away.

He laughs and exits.

Scene Two

Penelope   And you, gentlemen, this is my private hour and I would appreciate it if you could respect my privacy.

Dusty   Of course, Lady Raeburn, just before we go, do you mind if we can ask a couple of questions?

Dusty *gestures to* **Penelope** *to come and sit next to him by the window.*

Penelope   Gentlemen, is this really necessary?

Pidcock   You see, we know you were at the auction, however, there is a gap in your schedule which goes unaccounted.

Dusty   The time roughly falls during your 'private hour'.

Pidcock   Now if you don't want to remain a suspect, we need you to cooperate.

Pidcock *attempts to sit next to them but they get up and move away.*

Penelope   I understand . . . Very well . . . During my private hour I earn a little extra income making phone calls to lonely individuals and offer them . . . solace . . . and maybe a little bit more now and then.

Pidcock   Interesting, do you mind if I take that number, purely for the investigation . . . of course . . .

He laughs awkwardly.

Dusty   But why does a person like yourself need the money? I mean, you own a lot of land here, shouldn't you be entitled to its riches?

Penelope   How do you know this is my land?

Pidcock   I'm sorry, we must keep our sources confidential.

Dusty   That's right, Detective.

Pidcock   Otherwise Nora could get into a lot of trouble.

Dusty *looks in disbelief,* **Pidcock** *is slightly embarrassed.*

Penelope   Oh Nora, she is always looking out for me.

Penelope *sits* **Dusty** *on the chair as she rests on the arm rest.*

Pidcock   Isn't the countryside the first place you met Nora?

Penelope   Correct, upon my trips to the countryside I'd visit a local orphanage, she stood out from the rest.

Pidcock   You do a lot for charity?

Pidcock *rests his arm on the chair, however* **Penelope** *pushes it off, making* **Pidcock** *fall.*

Penelope   I try to, if it's not at an orphanage then it's the Sunnyside Care Home in town.

Dusty   Pardon?

Penelope   The Sunnyside Care Home caters to the sick and elderly. A little project away from my husband.

Pidcock   And what does Lord Raeburn do exactly?

Pidcock *places his foot on the table, which collapses and he falls.*

Penelope   He has a lot of dealings in foreign affairs and is always bringing clients to Raeburn Manor. Like our current guest Miss Anastasia Bramavich.

Pidcock   And what do you know about Miss Anastasia Bramavich?

Pidcock *goes to sit on the footstool, however* **Penelope** *kicks it away, causing* **Pidcock** *to fall onto the ground.*

Penelope   Not as much as my husband, only that she's a beautiful Russian heiress who had a particular interest in the painting.

Dusty   And let me guess, his business dealings are in private away from yourself and the staff.

Pidcock   That's enough, Dustin, you're speculating!

Penelope   Should I be worried?

Dusty   It's a little dubious, don't you think, my lady?

Pidcock   Dustin! I told you that there is nothing suspicious about Lord Raeburn requiring some alone time from his wife and the staff without being disturbed, while he does his business with attractive, young guests. It's preposterous!

Penelope (*worryingly*)   Actually, Detective, when you say it like that, it does make things seem rather precarious.

Dusty   Well, my dear, I wouldn't jump to conclusions, I'm sure there's nothing to worry about.

Pidcock   Well, that's the most sensible thing you have said, Dustin. Of course there's nothing to worry about . . .

Dusty *comforts* **Penelope**.

Pidcock   . . . But then again, you can never tell these days, one minute you're madly in love, they tell you they adore you, but really, they're lying . . . then the next thing you know, they're gone and you're left with nothing but pain and loneliness . . .

Penelope (*trembling*)   Ohhh, my goodness.

Dusty   Yes, Detective, I may have miscalculated, I think you've said enough.

Pidcock   Yes, Dustin is quite right, that is quite enough . . .

Beat.

. . . But then again, it's never enough. You think you've said all you can to keep them close but it's not enough, you begin to question. What happened? How it happened? Who am I? Where am I? What are you? Where are you? How are you? Who are you?

Penelope   Oh no, Henry! (*Sobs.*)

Dusty   Pidcock, you've made your point.

Pidcock   Of course, I think I've made my point clear . . .

Beat.

. . . But then again, what is the point? They leave you and life spirals out of control, the depression kicks in, so you turn to the drink because the drink helps, it helps you to forget them and it comforts you. Suddenly, years of marriage seem somewhat meaningless.

Penelope *sobs uncontrollably.*

Penelope   Nooo! (*Hysterical.*)

Dusty   Detective!

Pidcock   And you're worried about a painting when your marriage is on the brink! My goodness, what is the matter with you, woman, are you sick in the head, have you lost your mind? Are you crazy? (*Starts to strangle/shake* **Penelope**.) What is the matter with you?

Dusty   Detective, pull yourself together.

Dusty *pulls* **Pidcock** *off* **Penelope** *and starts to strangle/shake* **Pidcock**.

Penelope   Can't you see the poor man isn't well?

Penelope *pulls* **Dusty** *off* **Pidock** *and starts to strangle him instead.*

Pidcock   How dare you, get off my partner, you monster!

Pidcock *pulls* **Penelope** *off* **Dusty** *and starts to strangle her.*

Dusty   Detective, that is not how you treat a lady.

Dusty *pulls* **Pidcock** *off* **Penelope** *and starts to strangle* **Pidcock**.

Penelope   How dare you, I can handle myself.

Penelope *pulls* **Dusty** *off* **Pidock** *and starts to strangle him instead.*

Pidcock   Get off him.

Pidcock *pulls* **Dusty** *off* **Penelope**, *suddenly there's a stand off, they eye each other up then they all start to strangle each other.*

Lord Raeburn *enters in a flurry.*

Scene Three

Raeburn GOOD HEAVENS, WHAT IS THE MEANING
OF THIS NONSENSE?!

Pidcock Okay, Mrs Raeburn. Thank you for your time.
You've been very helpful.

Penelope Very well.

Lady Raeburn *exits.*

Raeburn Do either of you care to explain yourselves?

Pidcock My lord, there was just a simple
misunderstanding, isn't that right, Dustin?

Dusty Just a simple misunderstanding, my dear chap.

Raeburn I should hope so, we can't have you behaving like
this in Raeburn Manor.

Pidcock Of course not, I admit our methods are a little
unorthodox but we will be a lot more considerate in future.

Dusty Maybe now would be a good time for you to answer
a few questions. Is that okay with you, Lord Raeburn, or
should I say, Henry?

Dusty *sits down.*

Raeburn If you are attempting to infuriate me then try
harder because I will not stoop to your level.

Lord Raeburn *desperately tries to free his arms but is unable to.*

Pidcock Dustin, what are you doing?

Dusty Your interrogating has gotten us nowhere, now it's
my turn. Maybe if we riled him up a little bit, he might
reveal something.

Pidcock He is still the lord of the manor so be respectful
. . . I am sorry about him, my lord.

Raeburn   So you should be, you've both lost sight of what truly matters. You're too blinded by your own self-importance that you can't see where you're actually heading . . .

Lord Raeburn *walks into a piece of furniture and bangs his knee, he hobbles but tries to remain unfazed by it.*

Raeburn   Just wait until I tell your Chief about your misconduct, you won't have a leg to stand on.

Pidcock   Sir, we are so close to solving the case, please just give us a little more time.

Raeburn   Never, I am finally taking a stand.

Lord Raeburn *sits down.*

Pidcock   But sir, let's be reasonable.

Raeburn   I have been more than reasonable, now I'm putting my foot down.

Lord Raeburn *turns to put his feet up in an attempt to wriggle out.*

Dusty   What about your dealings in foreign affairs?

Raeburn   Miss Bramavich had a keen interest in the painting and offered a generous amount for it.

Dusty   You're really determined to sell Lady Penelope's painting, aren't you?

Raeburn   That's my painting, you imbecile.

Dusty   Oh, that's not what we heard.

Raeburn   How dare you! I will not stand for this!

Pidcock   I am so sorry about him, my lord, please let me take your coat and get you comfortable.

Raeburn   That won't be necessary.

Pidcock *removes* **Lord Raeburn**'*s jacket, in the process* **Lord Raeburn** *gets his arms tangled and stuck. He wriggles and writhes to try and get himself free.*

Pidcock   Sorry, sir, I didn't unbutton you . . . Hold still . . .

Raeburn   Oh give me that, I can manage on my own. Yes, it's clear to me that you've become too caught up in the mess you have created. You're at a loss, incompetent, restricted.

He attempts some more, until he realises he is stuck.

Lord Raeburn *stands up out of his chair.*

Dusty   All I am saying is that some people are quick to sell things that don't belong to them.

Raeburn   I haven't done anything of the sort.

Dusty   That's not what we have heard?

Raeburn   You are asking for it now, put 'em up.

Lord Raeburn *desperately tries to free his arms but is unable to.*

Pidcock   I am so sorry about all this, my lord.

Raeburn   Oh, keep your apologies, your Chief Constable will be hearing about this, that's for sure. Not only are you clearly struggling to untangle yourself, not only is *my* painting still missing, but you cannot insult me in *my* own home!

Dusty   Your home? That's not what we have heard?

Raeburn   That settles it!

Pidcock   Oh dear.

Raeburn   I've had it up to here with the pair of you!

Lord Raeburn *can only get his arms up mid-way.*

Pidcock   Oh, that's a relief, I thought it was a lot worse than that.

Raeburn (*screams*)   It is a lot worse than that . . . I've had it up to *here* with the pair of you.

Pidcock   Phew!

Again, **Lord Raeburn** *can only get his arms up mid-way, at this point he loses all composure and dances and jigs around the room to free himself.*

Raeburn   I've had it up to . . . I've had it up to . . . *hereeee* . . . I've . . . HEREEE YOU WON'T BE MAKING A FOOL OUT OF ME! . . . I've had it up to hereee!

There is a moment where **Lord Raeburn** *dances across the stage to free his arms. In the end he gives up.*

I've had it up to . . . I'm fed up with the pair of you. Yes, Detective, you have lost all composure . . . this must be awfully embarrassing for you . . . Don't you look ridiculous now.

Lord Raeburn *exits.*

Dusty   Well, it looks like that is the end of the road for us, Pidcock.

Dusty *grabs their hats, passes* **Pidcock**'s *across to him, gesturing for him to leave.*

Pidcock   Not necessarily, Dustin, if we are able to find this culprit before the Chief gets here then we can still keep our jobs and freedom.

Dusty   I know the chap's hiding something, I just know it, a love affair perhaps?

Pidcock   The lord is a respected member of the community, he is the last person on earth to be unfaithful and if you're not careful with what you say to him, then we are done for.

Dusty   You're right, Detective.

Pidcock We must keep our heads at all times, no funny business, no being distracted by any suspects or we can kiss our futures goodbye.

Scene Four

Enter **Anastasia Bramavich**.

Anastasia Well hello, darlings.

Dusty Oh my.

Pidcock Get ready to kiss our future goodbye . . . Hello. You must be Shagabich, Bramavic! Anastasia Bramavich.

Dusty That's a lovely name.

Anastasia Thank you, I'm Russian.

Pidcock Yes, I appreciate you're a busy woman but this won't take long.

Dusty We don't often get your people over here.

Anastasia Sure you do, us Russians are everywhere, except most of them shorten their name to 'fit in'.

Dusty I understand.

Anastasia The trouble with people fitting in is that it's very difficult to get them out.

Pidcock Well, if you ever need help getting them out, you know where we are . . .

Anastasia I tell you what. I'll tell you everything and we will see what else you can get out of me, how does that sound?

Dusty That sounds perfectly splendid for us, doesn't it, Pidcock?

Pidcock You can say that again.

Dusty   That sounds perfectly splendid for us, doesn't it Pidcock?

Anastasia   You boys seem a little flustered, why?

Pidcock   Vy?

Anastasia   Why?

Dusty   Why. She's saying 'why', you fool.

Pidcock   Why? (*More demanding.*) Because there's an important investigation underway and you need to tell me *why* you are here at Raeburn Manor?

Anastasia   Oh Detective, very stern, I'm impressed. I'm an antiques dealer, travelling the world to auctions and stately homes. I was having a nice little tour of your country, when I met Lord Raeburn. I told him I would do anything to get my hands on his . . . antiques. When he told me about the priceless painting I just couldn't resist, so he invited me to the auction and kindly offered me a room in the manor.

Dusty *nudges* **Pidcock**.

Dusty   So what other cities have you visited in Britain?

Anastasia   Oh, well of course there is London –

Pidcock   Of course.

Anastasia   . . . And there's Manchester, Birmingham, Liverpool and . . . (*Looks around the room.*) New Hat . . . Stand . . . Shire . . . New Hatstandshire.

Pidcock   Really?

Dusty   Hmm, how interesting.

Anastasia   But of course what use is visiting all these lovely places if you have no one to share it with?

Dusty   Well, if you ever want to share it with someone again /

Pidcock *nudges* **Dusty**.

Pidcock (*stuttering*)   I see . . . And . . . (*Clears throat.*) could you please tell us what you did on the day of the auction?

Anastasia   Of course, I woke up in the morning with my usual coffee and stayed in my room all day getting ready for the auction.

Dusty   And what else?

Anastasia *laughs, the others feel extremely hot under the collar.*

Pidcock   Come now, we can either do this the easy way or the hard way.

Anastasia   That is all I did, Detective.

Pidcock   Is there anyone who could confirm your whereabouts?

Anastasia   In my bedroom? I'm not that sort of girl, Officer! . . . Or am I?

Dusty/Pidcock   Well . . . I . . . Ermmm.

Dusty *and* **Pidcock** *are very hot under the collar.*

Anastasia   Now I have had it the easy way, how about you try it the hard way?

Dusty *and* **Pidcock** *share a look and cover their private areas with their hats.*

Anastasia (*yawning*)   I'm feeling very tired with all this questioning, so I'm going to have a little lie down. If you would like to know more then please join me . . . but be warned, it's so hot in there that I have to sleep with very, very little clothing . . . Goodbye, boys . . .

Anastasia *leaves.*

Dusty/Pidcock   Goodbye . . . (*Waving.*)

Pidcock *and* **Dusty** *are in a love trance with their hats still covering their private areas, despite their hands being by their side.*

Dusty   I think she stole my wallet.

Pidcock I think she stole my heart. We should really go and follow her . . . for the investigation.

Dusty It could be a trap.

Pidcock It would be a shame if someone walked into it . . .

Dusty It's a sacrifice I would be willing to make.

Pidcock I'll say.

Nora *enters.*

Nora Anyone for tea?

Nora *looks at how their hats are being propped up and faints.*

They run over to her and try to get her back on her feet, in doing so they have her bent on all fours, each of them at either side being very suggestive.

Enter **Roy.**

Roy Cooor blimeyyy, they're at it again! LORD RAEBURN!

Roy *exits.*

Dusty Quick, get her up, Pidcock.

Pidcock We need to get her to the window!

Dusty No, we can't do that to her again!

Pidcock We have no other choice.

The pair drag her towards the window and lift it up, then try and position her outside.

Dusty There must be another way.

Pidcock We can't risk the lord finding out about this.

Lord Raeburn *enters.*

Raeburn Find out about what exactly?

Dusty No, no, it's not what it looks like!

Raeburn   It looks to me you were about to throw the poor maid out the window.

Pidcock   My goodness, that's exactly what was about to happen.

They realise what **Pidcock** *has just said.*

Dusty   Pidcock!

Raeburn   I knew it! I just knew you were incapable of doing your jobs, that settles it!

Pidcock   No, please, Lord Raeburn!

Raeburn   Do you hear? It's over for you now. You two are finished. Come with me, Nora, you poor thing!

Nora   I know his secrets!

Raeburn   Thank you, Nora, but now isn't the time.

Lord Raeburn *pushes* **Nora** *out the window and closes it.*

Raeburn   You will lose your job and you will be straight back to jail.

Dusty   No, no, Lord Raeburn, don't be like that, let's talk about it.

Raeburn   You're finished, I tell you, finished!

Lord Raeburn *exits.*

Scene Five

Dusty   Nooo! We were so close!

Dusty *has a little meltdown.*

That's it, we're bloody done for. Well, it was nice working with you, Detective. I can't go back there I tell you, I just can't!

Pidcock   But surely being a master criminal like yourself you can break out of there or come up with a new plan to get yourself freed?

Dusty   It's not as easy as that, Detective.

Pidcock   You must have known the consequences of your actions.

Dusty   Well, yes, but . . .

Pidcock   But what? Those were your actions, weren't they?

Dusty   What do you mean?

Pidcock   You're not Dustin Wills at all, are you?

Dusty   What makes you say that, Detective?

Pidcock   Now it's time for me to do a little seducing, Dustin.

Dusty   You mean deduce?

Pidcock   Yes . . . I've been following the escapades of Dustin Wills for many years and there was one thing which startled me when you turned yourself in.

Dusty   Which was?

Pidcock   You turned yourself in. Dustin Wills would never have done such a thing.

You had me fooled early on, I'll give you that, but now it's become more clear. You see, all your theories and speculations are terrific, genius, but they weren't yours. Every single one came from a novel or a tale of the infamous Dustin Wills. You're nothing more than a Dustin Wills devotee. You're a person like myself, desperately trying to leave some kind of a legacy, but at least I'm not taking credit for someone else's accomplishments. You, sir, are a fraud!

Dusty   You're right.

Pidcock   Go on, admit it! Wait, what?

Dusty   You're right, I was infatuated with the tales of Dusty Wills that I was willing to take all the blame in the hope that I could become someone, anyone, but then I realised what I was in for and desperately tried to resolve it.

Pidcock   So it appears we both have a lot riding on this?

Dusty   It would appear so.

Pidcock   What's your real name?

Dusty   . . . Frank.

Pidcock   Of course. It's nice to meet you . . . Frank.

Dusty   I guess none of us are really our true selves, it really is an art being so deceptive.

Pidcock   Say that again.

Dusty   It is truly an art being so deceptive.

Pidcock (*realising*)   The Art of Deception . . . that's it!

Something clicks inside **Pidcock***'s head.*

Dusty   What's it?

Pidcock   Dustin, what was in the locked drawer when you opened it?

Dusty   Nothing, except a plaque that said 'COUNT VYMOROV'.

Pidcock   Oh, it all makes sense!

Dusty   Does it?

Pidcock   Of course, there's a reason why we were struggling to piece everything together. But the answer was staring at us the whole time.

Dusty   So what do we do now? Do what they normally do in the novels and gather all the suspects together to finally reveal the culprit?

Pidcock   Oh please, this isn't one of those Shoddy Detective plays.

They give a look to the audience.

We need to check one or two final things beforehand but we might have finally gotten to the bottom of this! Come with me.

They exit.

Scene Six

Enter **Pidcock** *and* **Dusty** *followed by other guests and workers.*

Pidcock   Right. We've gathered you all here because as you know, we have been trying to find the culprit who stole the infamous painting. Well, ladies and gentlemen, we can now confirm that the thief is in this very room.

Everyone gasps.

Yes, now brace yourselves because the truth is quite shocking. First up we have the gardeners.

Mick *and* **Roy** *enter.*

Dusty   They were our initial suspects because they had the easiest access to the painting that morning and an eyewitness saw Mick leaving the grounds.

Pidcock   Mick told us he went out that afternoon because he . . . what was it again, Mick?

Mick   Buying wood.

Pidcock   Ah yes, for a new garden fence. Now, you had our suspicions as we found no wood nor a refurbished fence.

Dusty   This also coincides with a luxury retreat to Spain staying at . . . where was it again, Roy?

Roy   Sunnyside Resort.

Dusty Ah yes, the Sunnyside Resort. Now, there was some truth in that, Roy, as you are staying at the Sunnyside Resort.

Roy That's my boy! Isn't my boy wonderful? Isn't my boy brilliant?

Dusty Only it isn't a resort in Spain but a care home on the edge of the town.

Roy Isn't my boy . . . an ungrateful little sod!

Mick I'm sorry father, but you've got to go!

Roy *grabs* **Mick** *around the earlobe and begins to drag him off stage.*

Roy You wait until I get you home, young man!

Dusty Not so fast, Roy, as you yourself have some explaining to do . . .

Pidcock You were the closest to the painting just before it went missing but you were a little preoccupied with something else it seems.

Dusty The clue was the flower arrangement. We were wondering what you were up to, then we found out where you were getting your little thrills, or should I say . . . frills!

Dusty *pulls out the pair of underwear from the plant pot.*

Pidcock Don't take notice of his humour, you could always turn the other cheek . . .

Dusty Well played, old chap.

Mick You randy old git! You wait until I tell your father about this!

Dusty/Pidcock His father?!

Enter even older gardener.

Oldest Gardener (*screeching*) He's done what?! Come here, young man.

*He grabs **Roy**'s ear and one by one they exit, groaning in pain.*

Dusty   During our talk with Lady Raeburn she revealed that she often does charity work for the Sunnyside Care Home in the village. With Mick's shifty antics, matched with his false pretenses, we put the two and two together.

Pidcock   He might have been successful if it wasn't for an eyewitness who saw him leave the grounds that morning.

Dusty   However, that eyewitness should never have seen him leave, as they were not at their usual station.

Pidcock   After doing some digging we uncovered an underground scandal, taking place here, in Raeburn Manor, which involved buying and selling stolen jewellery and antiques on the black market.

Dusty   It appears they made quite the business for themselves. Isn't that right, Bertha?

Pidcock *backs away from the door and hides behind the furniture, bracing for impact.*

Bertha   You what?

*She grabs hold of **Pidcock** and pulls him from behind, he screams.*

Pidcock   Oh god, no Bertha, please . . .

Bertha   I tell you I'm not a thief.

Dusty   Bertha, that may not be 100 per cent accurate as you became so enthralled in your work you began to get sloppy. If I hadn't noticed the diamond bracelet you wore when we first shook hands I would never have suspected it.

Pidcock   Then there was the perfume Mrs Wymore was wearing. I thought I recognised it from somewhere and I was right, I had smelt it before, not on a movie actress but, in fact, on you.

Dusty Bertha, you managed to secure a modest living, stealing from guests or trading jewellery for information. This is where you come into things, Mr Wymore.

Richard I told you, I make an honest living working in insurance. What are you gonna do, arrest me?

Pidcock Quite possibly, as you stole your wife's jewellery and claimed they were lost so she wouldn't contact the police meaning you could claim on the insurance before selling the jewellery on for a cheaper price without her knowing, thus doubling your fortune.

Richard Bertha, they're onto us, run away with me, we make a great team you and I.

Bertha I work alone!

Bertha *exits.*

Richard Please, Bertha, let me come with you!

Snaps to **Mary.**

Mary Nooo, Richard, how could you possibly leave me?

She sobs.

Dusty I am sorry, Mary.

Mary Oh, why do bad things always happen to good people?

Dusty Well, that's not entirely true, is it?

Mary I say, what could you possibly mean by that?

Pidcock Mary, it appears you have made a small fortune yourself at the expense of Lady Raeburn.

Mary No such thing, Penelope is a close friend of mine and I hold her dear to my heart.

Dusty Would a dear friend also use blackmail in order to prevent them from exposing something from that person's past?

Mary   I don't know what you mean.

Pidcock   You see, Mary, you have something of Lady Raeburn's that she holds in high regard, something in which she regularly gives you a large amount of money in order to keep it to yourself. This isn't a physical object but a secret. A secret you have known for many years and have been paid handsomely in order to remain hush about it.

Dusty   Nora, would you please come here for a moment?

Nora *enters.*

Dusty   Nora, dear, where did you grow up?

Nora   In an orphanage.

Dusty   Out in the countryside, which just so happens to be the place Lady Raeburn was sent all those years ago.

Nora   It's very coincidental, I'll give you that. She might have seen me when I was a baby.

Beat. They look at each other.

Pidcock   Oh, I have no doubt that she saw you Nora, as she is in fact your mother.

Nora   Lady Raeburn?

Dusty   Mary knew this as they were old friends but chose to blackmail Penelope to keep her secret hidden.

Nora   You blackmailed my mother, you evil witch!

Nora *chases* **Mary** *who screams and runs off stage.*

Mary   Oh no!

Richard   She went that way!

Nora   Hang on, I have a mother?!

Dusty   That is correct.

Nora   And my mother is one of the wealthiest people in the land?

Pidcock   Also correct.

Nora   And that crooked cow made me work for low pay for her for all those years?

Dusty   I know it seems a bitter pill to swallow but it is the reason why she brought you here, in order to keep a close eye on you and to make sure you had an education.

Nora   I'm educated enough to know my mother is an uptight count-try girl! Well, I won't tolerate this for any longer.

Nora *gets up and moves towards the door.*

Enough is enough, I have had enough of this place, I am leaving, I am . . .

Lord Raeburn *enters and hits* **Nora** *in the face with the door.*

Raeburn   What was that about Penelope?

Dusty   Nora, are you alright?

Nora   Oh no, don't worry, I am perfectly fine. (*She laughs hysterically.*)

Nora *staggers towards the window, opens it and throws herself out.*

Raeburn   I say, dear chaps, did I hear you correctly? Penelope has been fostering her own child under my very nose? I am appalled at this.

Dusty   Don't you give me that, you knew deep down about Penelope's past. You knew that once Penelope returned from her trip to the countryside, she would struggle to find a husband. This was your perfect opportunity to inherit the land and finally get status and riches you desperately desired.

Raeburn   How dare you! If I was really that shallow then why would I continue this façade for so long.

Pidcock   Why wouldn't you, you have land, wealth, priceless paintings. You have access to it all, at your fingertips.

Raeburn   Now, now, gentlemen, let's not be too hasty.

Dusty   You seemed particularly keen on a certain individual to have the painting and it wasn't Lady Raeburn, was it?

Raeburn   Now, now, gentlemen. I keep things strictly business.

Pidcock   Oh, I am sure you do, Lord Raeburn, as you discuss 'business' with this person regularly and often ask for tea and coffee to be brought to your room. However, Lady Raeburn and yourself don't drink coffee . . .

Dusty   The real question is, who is this mystery woman? Probably the only coffee drinker here . . .

Pidcock   The Ravishing Russian, Miss Anastasia Bramavich.

Enter **Anastasia**.

Dusty   Or should we just say ravishing.

Anastasia   I don't know what you mean?

Dusty   You're not Russian at all, are you? You are, however, impeccably talented at luring people in for your own personal gain. Now, there is only one criminal I know who has the exceptional capability of executing something like that and she is . . . The Scouse Seductress!

Anastasia (*native accent*)   Ah, the jig's up then . . .

Anastasia *exits*.

Dusty   My first clue was when I asked her which great cities she visited in Britain, and she said Manchester, Birmingham, Liverpool and New Hatstandshire. She made a big mistake . . .

Pidcock   Indeed she did. No foreigner in their right mind would visit Liverpool. It appears that Anastasia is, in fact, the Scouse Seductress, who used her charm to entice Lord Raeburn in the hopes she could secure the painting all for herself.

Dusty   So you can admit it, you don't deal in foreign affairs, just love affairs.

Pidcock   I told you, Dustin, he's not having an affair.

Raeburn   Alright, I admit it, I'm having an affair.

Pidcock   Just as I suspected!

Penelope *enters.*

Penelope   Henry, you beast!

Raeburn   Well, it looks like we have both been keeping secrets, isn't that right, darling? Perhaps you wanted to steal the painting to run off to the countryside with your own daughter?

Pidcock   Excuse me, but leave the accusations to us, thank you. How about you, Lady Raeburn, perhaps you wanted to steal the painting to run off to the countryside with your own daughter?

Penelope   That is preposterous, the painting belongs at Raeburn Manor and should remain so!

Pidcock   Penelope is right, it belongs in Raeburn Manor, with its rightful owner.

Raeburn   Thank you, Detective.

Pidcock   However, that is not you, and in fact you had some rather bad intentions for the painting, did you not, Lord Raeburn, or should I say Henry?!

Raeburn   How dare you.

Pidcock   You see, Dustin, there is a reason why Henry kept that plaque locked away in his desk for so long. It was probably the biggest clue we could possibly find.

Dusty   I beg your pardon?

Pidcock   What did that plaque say when you got it out?

Dusty   Count Vymorov.

Pidcock   Did it? Or were we just pronouncing it wrong? Not Vymorov but *Vy*-morov. You see, Nora was desperately trying to put all the clues together but couldn't. When she was in a state of unconsciousness she began to repeatedly ask 'why?', 'why?', so to bring her round we gave her a drink, which we probably gave a little too much of.

Dusty   But she asked for more, Detective.

Pidcock   Ahh, but did she? Or was she trying to tell us something? You see, Dustin, when I saw the plaque of the Lord's great grandfather, 'COUNT VYMOROV', I thought nothing of it, it was only when we met the phoney Russian that I started to realise.

Dusty   Realise what?

Pidcock   I realised that Lord Raeburn's great grandfather would have had to come to England at some point, where most likely they would have shortened their name in order to 'fit in' with society, they would firstly shorten their name from 'Vymorov' to . . .

Dusty   'Vymor'.

Pidcock   And remember the whole debacle with, 'Vy' and 'Why', try it now, without the Russian accent . . .

Dusty   'Wymor'.

Pidcock   You see, Dustin, Nora wasn't questioning 'Why?' or asking for 'more' whiskey, she was in fact trying to tell us that his real name is . . .

Dusty   WYMORE! Which means, the lord is secretly working with his brother to steal the painting, claim on the insurance and sell it on the black market.

Pidcock   Which is exactly what his very same brother was doing to his wife, Mary. It also explains the phone book with the initials 'D. W.', Dickie Wymore.

Penelope   Oh Henry, how could you?

Pidcock   The real question is, where is the painting?

Raeburn   I don't know, I'm innocent I tell you!

Pidcock   Right, you're under arrest for fraud and obstructing the course of justice.

Raeburn   I think not!

Lord Raeburn *throws* **Pidcock** *into the radio and 'Sing, Sing, Sing' by Benny Goodman starts to play.*

They all look at each other.

Raeburn   You'll never take me alive!

Chaos ensues, with all the characters coming on stage fighting each other.

Pidcock   THAT SETTLES IT! YOU'RE ALL UNDER ARREST!

Blackout.

Scene Seven

Newsreporter (*on radio*)   Caught at last, Detective Stuart Pidcock has made his mark by solving some of the biggest thefts in history. The painting was stolen by none other than Lord Henry Raeburn in an attempt to obtain the insurance money and later sell the painting on himself. Family and friends of the convicted are yet to issue a formal statement but they are said to be shocked and appalled by the news.

Our reporter was sent to interview a member of staff at
Raeburn Manor but they were sadly ravaged by the cook.
Unfortunately, the painting is yet to be recovered but at least
the criminals are safely behind bars.

Lights up on **Sweetheart**, **Dusty** *and* **Pidcock** *enjoying the*
success together.

Sweetheart   Gentlemen! Congratulations on catching the
thief, who'd have thought it was Lord Raeburn the whole
time. Hard luck you weren't able to find the actual painting
but some cases can't be explained.

Pidcock   I'll keep searching for it, sir.

Sweetheart   Oh, it'll be out of our reach now, no doubt it'll
turn up later on down the line. But for the meantime, you
have both held up your end of the deal. Dusty Wills,
providing you keep your nose clean you have your freedom.

Dusty   Thank you, Sweetheart.

Sweetheart   And Detective Pidcock, or should I say Chief
Inspector Pidcock, you are to be honoured in a ceremony for
your service to the police force. Congratulations once again.

Sweetheart *exits.*

Dusty   So your reputation is restored, you caught the bad
guys and proved you could solve the case.

Pidcock   It looks that way.

Dusty   And you couldn't have done it without your partner.

Pidcock   Let's not go that far –

Dusty   Oh, c'mon.

Pidcock   Maybe a little.

They both smile.

I guess you're a free man.

Dusty   I guess I am. What will you do now?

Pidcock I'm gonna go get my wife back. Maybe have a holiday, take a break from catching crooks. You?

Dusty I've always wanted to write a detective novel, I suppose I have first hand experience now.

Pidcock I suppose you do . . . You don't seem too enthusiastic . . .

Dusty No, I'm happy. I'm relieved if anything, just some things don't make sense to me, like why wouldn't Lord Raeburn just sell the painting for a good fortune, instead of faking its own theft and getting extra for the insurance?

Pidcock I will never nor want to understand the rich.

Dusty I don't know, it just seemed a bit too clichéd for me.

Pidcock My god, Dustin, what did you expect from an investigation?

Dusty I don't know, Detective, I was just hoping there would be a couple of plot twists and a more dramatic ending.

Pidcock I told you, it's not always like the novels.

Dusty Yeah, I guess you're right. Well, it's been a pleasure working with you, Detective.

Pidcock Take care . . . *Dusty.*

Dusty Take care, Pidcock.

Pidcock Please, call me Stu.

Dusty Take care, Stu.

They shake hands and smile. **Dusty** *turns to leave and begins to think.*

He stops in his tracks with his eyes calculating.

Dusty Stu? Hang on, when we first interviewed the gardeners, Roy said the only person he saw in the great hall was Bertha and stew.

Pidcock   I know, she must have been making stew for the auction.

Dusty   Lord Raeburn said Bertha made a beef tartare that day, not a stew, which means.

Dusty *turns around to see* **Pidcock** *holding a gun to him, he says nothing.*

Dusty   It was you all along.

Pidcock   You wanted your plot twist, Dustin, now here it is.

Dusty   But how did you do it?

Pidcock   When you work in this game long enough you begin to suss out certain people. When you manipulate their lies and dig up enough dirt, eventually no one knows what the truth is anymore.

Dusty   How did you know it would work?

Pidcock   It's the same way I knew you weren't really the notorious thief Dusty Wills . . .

Dusty   Because?

Pidcock   Because I am . . .

Beat.

I had you all convinced I was incapable of completing a simple task whilst carrying out one of the biggest heists yet.

Pidock *begins to head toward the painting, pulling away the blank canvas to reveal the artwork which was hidden under there the whole time.*

Now I have my painting and, thanks to you, a clear name. In return you have your freedom and a legacy, so I suggest you keep things quiet, enjoy life as the famous Dusty Wills and we go our separate ways . . . Now that truly is, the Art of Deception.

A train horn blows in the distance followed by music.

Pidock *exits.*

Dusty *exits in shock.*

Lights fade.

The end.

Methuen Drama Modern Plays

include

Methuen Drama Contemporary Dramatists

include

John Arden (two volumes)
Arden & D'Arcy
Peter Barnes (three volumes)
Sebastian Barry
Mike Bartlett
Clare Barron
Brad Birch
Dermot Bolger
Edward Bond (ten volumes)
Howard Brenton (two volumes)
Leo Butler (two volumes)
Richard Cameron
Jim Cartwright
Caryl Churchill (two volumes)
Complicite
Sarah Daniels (two volumes)
Nick Darke
David Edgar (three volumes)
David Eldridge (two volumes)
Ben Elton
Per Olov Enquist
Dario Fo (two volumes)
Michael Frayn (four volumes)
John Godber (four volumes)
Paul Godfrey
James Graham (two volumes)
David Greig
John Guare
Lee Hall (two volumes)
Katori Hall
Peter Handke
Jonathan Harvey (two volumes)
Iain Heggie
Israel Horovitz
Declan Hughes
Terry Johnson (three volumes)
Sarah Kane
Barrie Keeffe
Bernard-Marie Koltès (two volumes)
Franz Xaver Kroetz
Kwame Kwei-Armah
David Lan
Bryony Lavery
Deborah Levy
Doug Lucie

Alistair MacDowall
Sabrina Mahfouz
David Mamet (six volumes)
Patrick Marber
Martin McDonagh
Duncan McLean
David Mercer (two volumes)
Anthony Minghella (two volumes)
Rory Mullarkey
Tom Murphy (six volumes)
Phyllis Nagy
Anthony Neilson (three volumes)
Peter Nichol (two volumes)
Philip Osment
Gary Owen
Louise Page
Stewart Parker (two volumes)
Joe Penhall (two volumes)
Stephen Poliakoff (three volumes)
David Rabe (two volumes)
Mark Ravenhill (three volumes)
Christina Reid
Philip Ridley (two volumes)
Willy Russell
Eric-Emmanuel Schmitt
Ntozake Shange
Sam Shepard (two volumes)
Martin Sherman (two volumes)
Christopher Shinn (two volumes)
Joshua Sobel
Wole Soyinka (two volumes)
Simon Stephens (five volumes)
Shelagh Stephenson
David Storey (three volumes)
C. P. Taylor
Sue Townsend
Judy Upton (two volumes)
Michel Vinaver (two volumes)
Arnold Wesker (two volumes)
Peter Whelan
Michael Wilcox
Roy Williams (four volumes)
David Williamson
Snoo Wilson (two volumes)
David Wood (two volumes)
Victoria Wood

For a complete listing of
Methuen Drama titles, visit:

www.bloomsbury.com/drama

Follow us on X and keep up to date with
our news and publications

@MethuenDrama